Living
LANGUAGE

LANGUAGE AND SOCIETY

Susan Cockcroft

Hodder & Stoughton

A MEMBER OF THE HODDER HEADLINE GROUP

Acknowledgements

The author and publishers would like to thank the following for:

Copyright Text:

p. 9, D. McKinnon in D. Graddol, D. Leith, J. Swann (eds.) (1996) *English: history, diversity, and change*; p. 13, 'Shamed by your English?' advertisement, appears regularly in the press, including *The Guardian*, June 2000; p. 14, 'How to Get on in Society' by John Betjeman (1958); p. 15, job advertisements from *The Lady*, 21 August 2000; pp. 39–40, based on research by David Crystal, 1995, 1997, 1999; p. 72, *The Home of Today* (1930s); *Manners and Rules of Good Society (or Solecisms to be Avoided), 35th edition* (1913); p. 74, © *The Guardian*, 3 April 2000; p. 76, passage cited by D. Graddol and J. Swann, *Gender Voices* (Oxford: Blackwell 1989); p. 77, Women's Talk by 'Astra', in Dale Spender, *Man Made Language* (London: Rivers Oram/Pandora List, 1980); pp. 82–83, Conversation transcript from C. Stainton, *Interruptions; a marker of social distance* (OPSL Vol. 2, 1987); pp. 83–84, Exchange transcript from D. Schiffrin, *Approaches to Discourse* (Oxford: Blackwell 1994); p. 86, *The Guardian*, 31 May 2000; pp. 88–89, Courtroom exchange, Harris, in *Working with Language* by Hywel Coleman (Berlin, New York: Monton de Gruyter 1989); p. 89, extract from *A Room of Her Own*, Virginia Woolf (1925) cited in *Feminist Stylistics*, Sara Mills (Routledge 1995); p. 90, extracts from *Language and Masculinity* (Blackwell 1997) Johnson and Meinhof; p. 95, Anita Howarth and Teena Lyons, *The Mail on Sunday*, 6 August 2000; p. 103, *Independent Magazine*, August 2000; 104, first extract, *Guardian Weekend*, 5 August 2000; p. 104, second extract, *The Guardian*, 16 February 2000; p. 105, first extract, *The Independent*, 17 August 2000, p. 105, second extract, *Daily Mail*, 17 August 2000; pp. 106–107, Newspaper headlines: 1, *The Independent*, August 2000; 2, *Daily Mail*, August 2000; 3, *Daily Telegraph*, August 2000; 4, *Daily Telegraph*, 17 August 2000; 5, *The Times*, August 2000; 6, *Daily Mirror*, 17 August 2000; p. 107, *The Independent*, 17 August 2000; p. 109, *The Guardian*, Spring 2000; p. 109 Extract 1, *Friends Provident Group*, Summer 2000; Extract 2, *The Times*, 1 August 2000; Extract 3, *Tax Return Guide for the Year Ending April 2000*; p. 110, *The Guardian*, 3 April 2000; p. 114, D. Tannen (ed.), *Framing in Discourse* (Oxford: Oxford University Press 1993); pp. 114–115, Stephen Hawking's *A Brief History of Time* (Bantam Press 1998); p. 115, *The Guardian*, 3 August 2000; pp. 117–118, Harris, cited in *Working with Language*, by Hyweth Coleman (Berlin, New York: Mouton de Gruyter 1989); p. 120, *Advances in Spoken Discourse Analysis*, Malcolm Coulthard (Routledge: 1992); p. 122, John Sinclair and Malcolm Coulthard (1975); p. 123, adapted extract from Government publication detailing national literacy guidelines.

Copyright artwork:

p. 10, The Art Business; p. 17, William Labov, *Sociolinguistic Patterns* (Philadelphia, U. of Pennsylvania Press, 1984); p. 18, William Labov 1972, in Ronald Wardhaugh, *An Introduction to Sociolinguistics, Second edition* (Oxford: Blackwell 1992); p. 27, Hughes and Trudgill, *English Accents and Dialects* (London: Arnold 1979); p. 41, David Crystal, *The Cambridge Encyclopedia of Language* (© Cambridge University Press 1987), pp. 43, 51, 55, 57, David Crystal, *The Encyclopedia of the English Language* (© Cambridge University Press 1995); p. 87, Janet Holmes, *Women, Men and Politeness* (London: Longman 1995).

Every effort has been made to trace copyright holders of material reproduced in this book. Any rights not acknowledged here will be acknowledged in subsequent printings if notice is given to the publisher.

Orders: please contact Bookpoint Ltd, 78 Milton Park, Abingdon, Oxon OX14 4TD. Telephone: (44) 01235 827720, Fax: (44) 01235 400454. Lines are open from 9.00–6.00, Monday to Saturday, with a 24 hour message answering service. Email address: orders@bookpoint.co.uk

British Library Cataloguing in Publication Data
A catalogue record for this title is available from The British Library

ISBN 0 340 78099 1

First published 2001
Impression number   10 9 8 7 6 5 4 3 2 1
Year   2007 2006 2005 2004 2003 2002 2001

Copyright © 2001 Susan Cockcroft

Cover photo from The Ronald Grant Archive.
Typeset by Fakenham Photosetting Limited, Fakenham, Norfolk
Printed in Great Britain for Hodder & Stoughton Educational, a division of Hodder Headline Plc, 338 Euston Road, London NW1 3BH by J.W. Arrowsmith, Bristol.

Contents

Introduction

The book focuses on the complex subject of language and society (the academic study of this subject is called **sociolinguistics**). It aims to help you, as a student of English Language, to gain a clearer understanding of:

- the society you live in
- the people you meet
- the language you speak, hear, write and read.

All these make a difference to your own use of English.

So what do we mean by 'society'?

Despite former Prime Minister Margaret Thatcher's famous remark 'There is no such thing as society!', few people would deny that we are 'social animals', and have been so since our earliest days on the African plains, when *homo sapiens* chose to live in social groups, and to share shelter, food, and mutual protection from danger. Today the situation is different. Some people live alone by choice, while others select from a wide variety of *social groupings*, ranging from couples and single parent families to nuclear families, communes, shared flats or houses. Wherever they live, most people have regular *social contact* with other humans – at work, in school, on public transport, at the supermarket, the temple or church, in pubs and clubs, at the cybercafé . . . the list is endless. Today people know about what's happening in society by reading newspapers, surfing the net, watching television or listening to radio. Within seconds we can *communicate* with other humans almost anywhere in the world by telephone or the Internet.

Unless we are *really* determined to remain isolated from society, we are inextricably involved in it. Although we are individuals, we have an *effect* on other people, who in turn *affect* us, *influencing* how we speak, think, and act. This involvement was vividly described nearly 400 years ago by John Donne, poet turned preacher, who wrote:

No man is an Island entire of itself; every man is a piece of the continent, a part of the main.

Society *does* exist, and we are all part of it!

Talking about language and society

Some key terms

Academic jargon can be annoying; nevertheless, it's important that you learn some of the key linguistic terms used in the study of language and society. You have already met the word *sociolinguistics* (note the link with *sociology*); an equally important term is **idiolect**. This is the unique way each of us has of using language, and it includes everything from the words we choose and the slang we prefer, to our accent and our particular tendency to gabble or mumble when we've got something important to say. The characteristic language use of a particular *social group* (eg teachers, teenagers, computer experts, baseball players) is called a **sociolect**.

A few more key terms you need to know at this stage are:

- speech community
- social contexts
- communicative competence
- social network
- linguistic variables.

We'll start off with some explanations immediately. (There will be other terms to take on board later when we look at particular topics, but they can wait for now.)

Speech community means a group of people who share a similar social experience, and hence share similar vocabulary and grammar. They could be people who live in the North of Scotland in an isolated fishing village. They might be fans of heavy metal or jazz living at opposite ends of the country. They might be local football supporters, or supporters of Manchester City from around the world – but *each person* would be part of a particular and unique speech community.

The number of people involved doesn't matter – the common language experience is what's important. Friendship groups, neighbourhood groups, work-based associations – all could be described as speech communities. And most of us are part of more than one – probably several – speech communities.

Sometimes there are tensions and conflicts between the language practices of different groups: for example, playground 'gangs' in primary school (each with their own secret codes); or attitudes to language (eg swearing) which may vary among different generations. When people meet, talk, consult, ask advice, argue, discuss problems or make plans, their *exchanges* will take place *within* a **social situation** (e.g. family meal, doctor's office, classroom, supermarket, job interview, restaurant).

Linguists describe these situations as **social contexts**, and they make an enormous difference to the way we actually use language. For example, the social context of the following situations determines (consciously or not) our language choices: we avoid taboo language *at home*; we give the doctor clear information about a health problem *in the consulting room*; we are polite *at the job interview* for the position we want!

ACTIVITY 1

1 Think of all the social groups or speech communities *you* are part of, and write them down. Beside each group jot down any words or expressions (or even grammar) which are special to that group. How many examples have you noted for each? Are some harder to characterise than others?

2 The following words come from semantic/lexical fields linked with a particular speech community or communities. Try to identify the speech community which uses each one (there are approximately 32):

double toe-loop combination jump	e-commerce	customers	editorial	NASA	BSE
conditioning treatment	focus group	statement	dressage	striker	scan
design specifications	spreadsheet	footlights	diocese	mulch	tort
anabolic steroid	conveyance	pirouette	shuttle	SATS	gig
reverse thrust	milk quota	turnover	torque	whisk	ace
silver service	zoom lens				

Communicative competence is the term for someone's ability to use appropriate language within a particular speech community. To do this we must recognise the community's linguistic 'rules' (*norms*), and how far changes can be made (*variations*) to fit any new situations. Note that *competence* has a particular meaning here, which is different from its usual one (ie that someone does a job well). It means that someone *knows* and can *use* the language of a particular community. As children gradually develop spoken language skills, they acquire **communicative competence**.

The term **code** can mean anything from a secret method of communication used by military intelligence (such as the Enigma code in World War 2) to secret languages invented by children to keep adults ignorant of their plans (eg 'talking backwards', cited by David Crystal or *eggy peggy language*). Today *code* can also mean 'appropriate choice of clothes'; restaurants, hotel bars and clubs may have a *dress code* (eg 'smart casual: no jeans, no T-shirts, no baseball caps', seen recently in a Westmorland hotel).

To sociolinguists the term *code* has a specific meaning: *a variety or style of spoken or written language used in a particular social context*. We all use a variety of linguistic codes in everyday conversation, and **codeswitch** almost without thinking as we adjust to new social situations (eg chatting casually to a friend in class, then responding to a complicated question from the teacher or lecturer). If you are bilingual, you probably **codeswitch** from one language to another in casual conversation, without even being aware you're doing it!

ACTIVITY 2

Chart *your own* range of code switches over the course of one day. Compare your findings with others in your group. Use the table below to help you.

You and your codeswitching		
	style?	language? (bi-lingual)
parent	y/n	y/n
sibling	y/n	y/n
friend	y/n	y/n
bus driver	y/n	y/n
teacher	y/n	y/n
employer	y/n	y/n
elderly relative	y/n	y/n
taxi driver	y/n	y/n
shop assistant	y/n	y/n

Social networks are the connections one individual has with other individuals or groups. (Indeed, a popular term today for making sure you meet the 'right people' at a party is *networking*!) The term came originally from the field of anthropology. *Social networks* frequently cut across class boundaries, and measuring the relative strengths of the networks can tell us a lot about individual members of *speech communities*. For example, one person's social networks may include: family; friendship group(s); fellow class members; sports club; drama group; church or similar religious group; Internet chat-room.

There are different ways of describing *social networks*, depending on the differences in people's informal social relationships. For example, if your best friends are also members of your extended family *and* you all work together *and* socialise together, you would be part of a **dense social network**. If the members of your network interact with each other in more than one context (at work, playing badminton, at church), it is called a **multiplex network**. If, on the other hand, you meet a wide variety of people who don't know each other, yours is a **loose social network**.

Here's an example of a *loose social network*: a friend of yours does aerobics with you, but you don't know her colleagues at work; your friends where you work part-time don't know your fellow students; you spend time at weekends with people who live locally, not with your college friends ... and so it goes on – a *loose social network*, with you at the centre.

We are all *influenced* in the ways we use language by our experience of social networks, and are continually adjusting register, vocabulary, even pronunciation, as we move from one *speech community* to the next.

ACTIVITY 3

Draw a spider diagram with you at the centre. Each 'leg' represents a speech community which you are part of. At the end of each 'leg' write down a few words which are particularly identified with that speech community (so 'family' might include *parent, brother, sister, home, washing up* etc; 'friends' might include *gossip, music, sharing, sport* etc). An example is shown below.

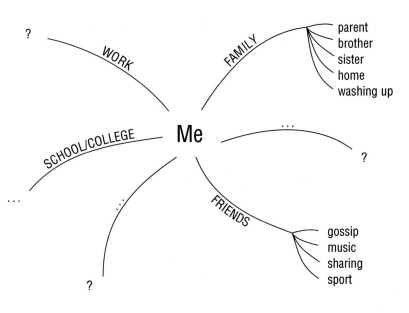

Linguistic variables are features of spoken language which *vary* from individual to individual, depending on factors like age, gender, status and social context. An example of a linguistic variable is the /ng/ consonant form used at the end of words like *running*. In Norwich this is pronounced in two ways: *running* or *runnin'*. In 1974 a linguistics researcher, Peter Trudgill, studied Norwich residents' differing pronunciations of '-ing' (*running/runnin'*). He tabulated his findings, taking into account the *social class* and *gender* of his subjects, and found that women and men in the higher social classes preferred '-ing' to '-in'. He deduced that the regional pronunciation (*runnin*) had less prestige than the Received Pronunciation form (*running*). So Trudgill's study is an example of a *linguistic variable* forming the basis of a research project.

Another example of sociolinguistic research based on a *linguistic variable* is the famous American linguist William Labov's investigation (1966) of /r/ usage in New York department stores, which we shall be looking at in more detail later in this chapter.

Approaches to language study

Micro- and macro-sociolinguistics are terms used by sociolinguists to describe the two contrasting ways of approaching their subject. If you focus on the way *society influences the way people use language* (through social variables like gender, class, age), this is called **micro-sociolinguistics**. If you focus on *what societies do with language* (investigating speech communities or attitudes to language use), this is called **macro-sociolinguistics**. In the course of the book we shall be looking at examples of both approaches.

ACTIVITY 4

Your task is to investigate a *speech community* (less daunting than it sounds!) Choose *one* speech community that you're part of yourself (eg one of your A level classes, a friendship group, a sports club or band etc). Listen to the normal conversation within this particular community over a period of approximately a week, but try not to be too obvious about it. (William Labov realised that people did not speak naturally if they were aware of people recording them and called this the **observer's paradox**.)

Note down, under the following headings, what characteristic language features you can remember (preferably, do this at the end of each day):

1 **Vocabulary:** was it *specific* to your chosen group (eg subject specific, use of slang, taboo language or dialect)?
2 **Non-standard grammar or syntax:** how frequent was it (eg '*We was late for the match*' [plural subject, singular verb]; '*I never did nothing*' [double negative])?
3 **Code-switching:** were there any examples of this (vocabulary or grammar) taking place in your chosen group?

Write a brief report of your findings using the headings above.

NB If you have the chance to tape-record some of the conversations within your speech community, the spoken data would form an excellent basis for an investigation.

After the introduction, what's next?

The book is divided into three sections, with two chapters in each section. Each section focuses on three important aspects of language and society.

Chapters 1 and 2 Attitudes to English at Home and Abroad

Chapter 1 explores the way speakers of English feel about their own language in its written and spoken forms. It shows how these attitudes are determined by *social factors*, as well as by individual judgements, and how these judgements, influenced by the media and the education system, are linked with *political, social* and *economic power*.

Chapter 2 investigates English as a world language, its advantages and disadvantages, and people's attitudes towards it. There will also be some detailed exploration of *different Englishes*, their use, and how people regard them.

Chapters 3 and 4 English and the Self: Representations of Difference

Chapter 3 and **Chapter 4** both focus on the ways in which the English language is used by people to express themselves as *individuals* within the context of society. We all have a sense of *self*, expressed in our *idiolect* (spoken language) and *style* (written language). These two chapters explore the particular effects of *age* and *gender* on the expression of individual *identity* in language, showing a wide range of *differing* responses.

Chapters 5 and 6 English in Everyday Life: Norms and Variations

Chapter 5 and **Chapter 6** provide an in-depth study of some of the range and variety of English used in everyday life today. Chapter 5 focuses on *new developments* in written and spoken English resulting from new technologies (computer language, text messaging, the Internet). We shall look particularly at the language of the media, business and public information. Chapter 6 focuses on more familiar areas of *occupational* variation (law, medicine, education), taking into account the current effects of new technology, and looking towards future developments. Both Chapters 5 and 6 will provide opportunities for you to have 'hands on' experience in analysing and evaluating language *in use*.

1 English at Home

What do we mean by 'attitude'?

Attitude can mean anything from a physical position or angle to a personal viewpoint or 'habitual mode of thought and feeling'. In casual conversation there can be even more meanings, depending on the context; 'She's got an *attitude* problem' (negative connotation) or 'He's cool – he's got *attitude*!' (positive connotation). In the world of sociolinguistics, however, the term is used to describe *personal and public opinion(s) about language*.

Where do these attitudes come from?

It's difficult to tell. Most of us don't stop to wonder, unless challenged, where our *own* opinions come from, never mind public opinion in general. Indeed, are our opinions really our own, or have we absorbed them from the world around us? Are they acquired from family and friends? From school or from the media? *When* are these attitudes acquired? At an early stage of language development, or much later? Do attitudes ever change? Which influences *change* people's attitudes?

We shall be looking for some answers to these important questions in the rest of this chapter. The following activity will start off the process.

ACTIVITY 5

Working in pairs, your task is to:

1 *Read* the following statements carefully (some are made up, some are actual quotations).
2 *Decide* what you think the speakers were trying to say about language in each statement.
3 *Write down* your individual or joint responses to each statement.

Example: Statement 1 *seems to show* that the speaker thinks a Birmingham accent is inferior, and it made her feel inferior. When she lost her job, she assumed this was the reason. *Your response* might be: 'My parents come from Birmingham so I really like the accent – I don't care what people think about it.'

Statements
1 'I lost my job because of my Birmingham accent.'
2 'Why can't the BBC use Queen's English speakers like they used to?'
3 'He's only got to open his mouth and he lets himself down.'

4 'We couldn't offer her a job – her spelling and handwriting were atrocious!'

5 'I can't stand being called *visually impaired* – I just can't see as well as I used to . . .'

6 'I wish I didn't have a local accent.' 'Oh, I really like yours – can't stand mine though!'

7 'The refuse disposal operatives had difficulties avoiding the raised person-hole covers in the street.'

8 'It is impossible for an Englishman to open his mouth, without making some other Englishman despise him.' (George Bernard Shaw, 1912)

9 'You should hear his language – you can tell what sort of person he is!'

10 'When I mark essays I insist on different *from* not different *to*!'

11 'I can't stand all these Americanisms you hear on the box all the time.'

12 'I really love a Scottish accent!' 'Yes, but I hate Glaswegian – you can't understand a word they say!'

13 'He told me to make sure that the motherboard was securely attached to all the ports, but I hadn't a clue what he meant.'

14 'Linguistic prescriptivism, established in the eighteenth century, was consolidated in the nineteenth century by scholars' obsessive interest in diachronic phonological variation within the Indo-European group of languages. Today we prefer descriptive linguistics, though there remain profound differences of approach between the systemic functional methodology and the transformational generative grammar tradition.'

ACTIVITY 6

Below is one linguist's suggested list of the kinds of favourable and unfavourable judgements people make about other people's English.

'I think the way s/he uses English is . . .'

1 correct/incorrect
2 beautiful/ugly
3 socially acceptable/socially unacceptable
4 morally acceptable/morally unacceptable
5 useful (for a particular purpose)/not useful
6 appropriate/inappropriate (for the context)
7 not controversial/potentially controversial (could offend)

(Source: D. McKinnon in D. Graddol, D. Leith, J. Swann (eds.) (1996) *English: history, diversity, and change*, p.342)

Look back at Activity 5. Can you match the statements in that activity with McKinnon's list above?

So what aspects of English do people make judgements about?

People hold strong views about their own and others' use of English in the following areas:

- accent
- dialect
- 'standard' and 'non-standard' English
- political correctness
- non-native speakers of English
- mistakes in spelling and punctuation
- social class
- prestige

- power
- jargon
- the 'complaint tradition' (English has gone from bad to worse!).

So what are the reasons for this? Where do these attitudes come from? Let's look for some explanations now.

It's all to do with power ...

Human history tells us that in any society some people (whether as individuals or in groups) will have more *power* than the rest. This power may simply come because they are physically stronger and can protect their dependents and their property; they may be more powerful because they possess more wealth (land, possessions, gold, water, oil or technology – whatever commodity is valued in their society). Others acquire power because they are political or religious leaders (Monarch, President, Prime Minister, Party Leader, Chief Priest, Dalai Lama); in particular cultures specific individuals may be powerful because they have particular skills and talents.

Most societies are also *hierarchical* (ie stratified or *ranked in order of power*), and Britain is no exception. From Anglo-Saxon times onwards, English society could be described as a power 'pyramid', with the monarch and the aristocracy at the top, Parliament, the merchant and manufacturing classes in the middle, and everyone else at the base. The rise and expansion of the middle classes has changed the situation to some extent, but there remains a social hierarchy in Britain today.

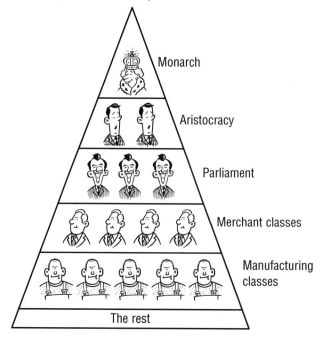

So is there a connection between social, political and economic power, and attitudes to the English language?

Virtually all the statements cited in Activity 5 reflect people's concerns about the fact that language is an *indicator of social power* (or lack of it). The way we speak – even the way we write – tells other people of our place in the social hierarchy. In turn, we make judgements about other people, *possibly* based on simple preference, but *probably* based on our perception of their *power* and *status*. For example, children in the Midlands and North can be quick to make negative judgements about new classmates from the South with a different accent ('She's a snob!'), the assumption being that her accent suggests *social status and power*. Similarly it is assumed that people whose accent is non-regional ('public school', 'Oxford accent', 'BBC accent') are rich and have power in society. *Accent stereotyping*, sometimes used for comic purposes but also reflecting social attitudes to power, occurs all the time in television advertising, 'soaps' and sitcoms.

ACTIVITY 7

Write down as many examples from television as possible of 'assumptions' about the relationship between language and power. For example, how many times did you identify a Northern accent being used? Was it used by someone reminiscing about their working-class childhood? Was it heard in a pub? Was it used by a criminal, a lawyer, a doctor or a teacher? Another example – what kind of goods or services was RP (Received Pronunciation) used

to advertise? What jobs did characters in sitcoms with RP/BBC accents have?

(Earlier power stereotypes in television include the Harry Enfield 'upper-class twit' type who advertises phones; Margot, the drawling anti-heroine of *The Good Life*; and the socially aspiring Hyacinth Bouquet and her imitators in *Keeping Up Appearances*.)

Language: the thermometer of social mobility

Language is influenced by those in positions of public power – people whose names we see when we open the newspaper or watch the television news. Power in today's society is not just located among the traditionally rich – wealthy land-owners, business men and industrialists. Media moguls and sports heroes, fashion designers and advertising executives all possess power. As a private *individual* you can be rich and famous as well as powerful if you win the lottery, become a millionaire, commit certain kinds of crimes or are involved in high-profile scandal. In the *public domain*, linguistic power can be exerted by people like the Chief Inspector for

Schools (eg influencing 'education speak' with terms like *SATS, literacy hour* etc); or genetic engineers (who have introduced us to genomes and genetic coding); or film directors (like Stephen Spielberg); and authors like Stephen King (*The Shining*), Roald Dahl (*Charlie and the Chocolate Factory*) and J. K. Rowling (the *Harry Potter* books which include the famous game, *quidditch*).

Since most people in positions of power have ready access to the media (hugely powerful by definition), it follows that *public attitudes to language* may be affected by the views from the 'top' of the power pyramid! Prince Charles's views on standard English are frequently quoted.

What other factors affect our judgements about language?

Not all our attitudes to language (our own as well as other people's) are linked with the power pyramid and our place in it. We like to be successful communicators because it's an important part of our self-esteem. Our *idiolect* is linked with our identity, our sense of *self*. Hence we judge ourselves ('I wish I could take that back!', 'Why do I make an idiot of myself as soon as I start to talk in public?', 'I should have checked that letter before I sent it . . .'). Feelings of *linguistic insecurity* can rapidly extend to feelings of social inadequacy, and worries about other people's linguistic judgements return ('Does she make people think she's got more status than me because of her accent?', 'Do I stand out like sore thumb in this group?', 'They make me feel really anxious when they're all talking business.', 'If I exaggerate my accent, will they take more notice of me?'). These kinds of feelings (conscious or unconscious) are a significant aspect of people's *attitudes to language*. The following advertisement powerfully demonstrates this linguistic insecurity.

ACTIVITY 8

1 Do *you* make judgements about people on the basis of how they talk? Think of two people you first met some time ago, or saw on television. As far as possible, try to recall your *initial impression* of the way they spoke, basing your judgement on their *idiolect, accent, voice, vocabulary, use of SE or non-SE*. Do you feel the same about the way they speak now they are more familiar? Have you changed your mind at all? Try to work out explanations for any change in your attitude. Compare notes with other people.

2 Collect examples from newspapers of people's attitudes to language (eg articles on accent, letters to the editor about usage etc).

3 Look at the advertisement *Shamed By Your English* below. Pick out the words associated with *power* which are intended to make the reader feel that the course will help him or her.

We are now ready to explore in detail some of the reasons for people's *attitudes* to language, focusing in particular on *social class, accent and dialect, standard and non-standard usage* and *political correctness*.

Language and social class

In this section we shall explore attitudes to language and *social class*, including the research of important British and American sociolinguists such as Basil Bernstein, William Labov, Peter Trudgill, and James and Lesley Milroy, among others.

Social class: a definition

How do we define *social class*? The official scheme divides people into different categories according to their *occupation* and their *income*. This kind of categorisation is crucial to the advertising industry, for example, who need to target their persuasion on exactly the right occupational and income group. Because occupation is a key indicator of social class, as employment patterns change, there will be movement between so-called social classes. Indeed, poverty and unemployment can topple people into the *underclass*, regardless of their previous educational, occupational or social status. But for us (and for sociolinguists) the key question is – how does social class affect people's language use?

The immediate answer seems to be that people's perception of social class differences is usually *stereotyped*. It tends to be based on pronunciation (**accent**), vocabulary (**lexical choice**), appropriate level of formality (**register**) and standard or non-standard usage (**grammar**, **spelling** and **punctuation**). There are further complications: judgements about class and status are made by people at *all* levels of society, and usages disliked by one social group (**stigmatised forms**) may be entirely acceptable to another group! Some people – often women (more of this in Chapters 3 and 4) – deliberately choose what they think is *more prestigious* language to impress others and imply superior status. The linguistic term for this is **hypercorrection**.

The television character Hyacinth Bouquet hypercorrects all the time; her exaggerated RP accent, together with her anxious desire to be seen as socially refined, makes for good situation comedy. The late Poet Laureate, John Betjeman, gently mocks a 1950s version of lexical hypercorrection in the poem *How to Get On in Society* (1958), in which he dissects the social aspirations of the 'lady of the house', who wants to do everything 'right' (from silver and napkins, to cakes and pudding). Unfortunately everything she says makes her more and more middle class, and less and less the upper-class hostess she longs to be!

Phone for the fish-knives, Norman
As Cook is a little unnerved;
You kiddies have crumpled the serviettes
And I must have things daintily served . . .

Now here is a fork for your pastries
And do use the couch for your feet;
I know that I wanted to ask you –
Is trifle sufficient for sweet?

Nancy Mitford and Alan Ross, writing at the same time as Betjeman, took a slightly different angle on linguistic social aspiration in their book *Noblesse Oblige* (1956), a series of essays about the differences between middle- and upper-class English usage. For example, they pointed out that U (upper-class) speakers talked about *writing paper*, *looking-glass* and *pudding*, whereas non-U (non-upper-class) speakers described the same objects as *note-paper*, *mirror* and *sweet*! Apparently, in the 1950s *social judgements* were made about people on the basis of their vocabulary choice.

It's worth noting that the upper-class Mitford and the middle-class Betjeman, who both *seem* to mock linguistic snobbery, actually perpetuate it.

ACTIVITY 9

Does someone's vocabulary choice *today* reflect social aspiration or indicate social status? One word that has changed status is *loo*; once an upper-class euphemism, it no longer signals social superiority because many people use the term. Can you think of any words used today to imply 'superior' social status? The extracts below are advertisements taken from a recent edition of *The Lady* (21 August 2000). This is a weekly magazine (founded in 1885) addressed to employers of *'Couples Cooks and Chefs Daily Cleaners Valets and Butlers Maternity Nurses Private Secretaries Housekeepers and Maids Nannies and Governesses Gardeners and Chauffeurs House and Estate Managers'*.

Is there any *linguistic* evidence of attitudes to social class in the vocabulary of the advertisements?

1 COUPLE REQUIRED
Aged approx. 50 yrs, to help maintain country house in Gloucestershire, as handyperson and housekeeper. Accommodation provided. These positions are full time.

2 HOUSEKEEPER/NANNY
Suffolk country house needs dedicated, happy, capable lady to help busy family. Twins 5 years, dogs, cats. Two cleaners already employed. Must be able to join, lead team to maintain high standards of household. Must be able to take sole charge. Driver. Non-smoker. Experience and qualifications advantage. References. Self-contained flat, car.

3 BATTERSEA
Titled couple seek mature House Keeper to help run their home. Must be child-friendly as newborn twins due Dec! (Live-in nanny also emp). Cooking skills not necc. Separate accommodation, alt. W/Es free.

4 AU PAIR CAMBRIDGE
3 girls (6, 3, baby). Must drive. Car provided. Start ASAP.

What can we learn about language and social class from sociolinguistic research?

By tracing a roughly chronological progression through the work of major researchers (eg Bernstein, Labov, Trudgill, the Milroys and Cheshire) we can identify the key issues, both past and present, in the area of *language and social class*. Significantly, accent and dialect, standard and non-standard usage are central to much of this research.

Basil Bernstein

Basil Bernstein, a former teacher, became one of the most influential British sociolinguists, researching issues of language and class in the context of education, and focusing particularly on *grammar* and *lexis*. He used the terms **'restricted'** and **'elaborated' codes** (see below) to describe what he saw as the differences between working-class and middle-class children's spoken language (ie their grammatical and lexical choices), but his ideas were immediately controversial, and have remained so ever since.

The reason for this was Bernstein's **deficit (or deficiency) hypothesis** (1961). He suggests that working-class – and especially lower working-class – children do badly at school because they use **restricted code** at home (ie short, simple and often incomplete sentences, limited vocabulary, frequent use of 'you know' etc). They have little understanding of **elaborated code** (complex sentences, use of subordination, extended vocabulary, use of the first person *I*) used by teachers who tend to be middle class. This accounts for these children's poor performance.

Despite much public outcry, some other sociolinguists agreed with Bernstein; as a result, language enrichment and remedial programmes for working-class children were set up to overcome these supposed *deficits* (eg Operation Headstart in the USA). Bernstein refined his ideas further, and came up with a more focused differentiation between what he now called **position-oriented or closed families** (working class) and **person-oriented or open families** (middle class). Again, his intention was to help what he perceived to be linguistically disadvantaged children. He suggested that the language of *position-oriented* or *closed families* (as demonstrated by the television sitcom *The Royle Family*) was:

- *personal* (close physical contact among family members)
- *context-bound* (shared surroundings, little movement beyond family situation)
- likely to share *common assumptions*
- inclined to *imply* rather than *spell out* meaning.

For example: position-oriented language

" 'You know what I mean?' I said to Mary, 'What do you mean by that?' she said 'Ask him, he knows what's what on this one.' 'Oh does he,' I said, 'well he'd better be letting me know what's on his mind or I'll be after him.' Pass me that, will you, before I forget it?"

The language of *person-oriented* or *open families* (as demonstrated by Basil in *Fawlty Towers*), however, was:

- more *impersonal*
- *context-free* (less dependent on surroundings for interpretations)
- *less likely* to assume *shared attitudes* and views.

For example: person-oriented language

"Could you let me know your plan for that meeting? Is it cancelled or not? What excuse are you proposing to make, and who do you expect to do your dirty work? It just isn't right to let people down when they've been expecting some answers about company policy."

In the *first* made-up example the close relationship between speakers means that they assume a common knowledge of the topic of conversation and can be imprecise (*what I mean, that, what's what, this one, it, what's on his mind*). Much is implied (the speaker is confident of her relationship with the listener), and sentences are short and simple. In the *second* example everything has to be explained (*meeting, cancelled, people, answers, company policy*), there is less sense of a personal relationship, syntax is more complex and uses subordination.

What is interesting about Bernstein's theories is that *everyone* uses *elaborated* and *restricted* code at different times in their life, and experiences *open* and *closed* or *person-* and *position-oriented* family situations. Bernstein was right in what he observed, but people's language usage is less fixed and more on a linguistic and social continuum than his theories allowed for.

William Labov

William Labov, the distinguished American sociolinguist, promptly challenged Bernstein's *deficit hypothesis*. He had studied the everyday speech (**vernacular**) of black working-class youths in New York, (*Language in the Inner City*, 1966), and was able to show that Black American Vernacular, far from being 'limited', could readily communicate abstract ideas (eg arguments about the existence or otherwise of God) using complex logic. The language may have been *non-standard*, but it was *not* 'restricted' in Bernstein's sense (personal, context-bound etc).

Labov undertook, and continues to undertake, other important sociolinguistic investigations, many of which research people's use of different **phonological variables** according to *social class*. We shall look at two of his major studies.

New York department stores study (Saks Fifth Avenue, Macy's and S. Klein), 1972

Probably Labov's most famous early investigation, this study explored the link between the incidence of /r/ pronunciation and *social class*. The sociolinguistic description of different *levels* in society is **social stratification** (eg *strata* as in geology). In New York the **phonological variable** /r/ in *cart* [carrrt] and *guard* [garrrd] is prestigious, whereas in British English the reverse is true; (/r/ pronunciation is used as a comic stereotype of 'rural' speech as in '*oo arr Farrmer Georrge*'.

Labov visited three New York department stores, Saks, Macy's and S. Klein, catering for upper-, middle- and lower-class social groups respectively. In the guise of a customer he asked staff the same question: 'Excuse me, where are the … ?' (knowing that the answer would be *on the fourth floor*). Pretending not to hear the response, he said 'Excuse me?' whereupon the subject responded emphatically 'Fourth floor!' Thus the interviewer was able to record *casual* as well as *emphatic* use or non-use of /r/.

He found that the higher the social class of the store's clientele, the more frequent the use of the prestige /r/. The bar graph below shows for each department store: a) the number of people who responded; b) the percentage of people using **all** /r/ pronunciation; c) the percentage of people using **some** /r/ pronunciation.

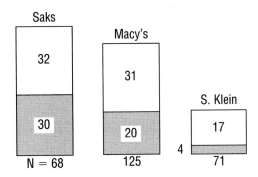

Overall stratification of (r) by store. Shaded area = % all (r-1); unshaded area = % some (r-1); % no (r-1) not shown. N = total number of cases.

Graph from p.51 William Labov, *Sociolinguistic Patterns* (Philadelphia, U. of Pennsylvannia Press, 1984)

a Select one of the three stores. Invent the complete dialogue between Labov and the store assistant starting with his key question, and using as many (r) pronunciations as you think appropriate.

b Note that Labov only asks store **staff**, not other customers. Why do you think this is?

Martha's Vineyard, 1972

Labov investigated differing pronunciations of certain vowels by Martha's Vineyard residents, also in the context of **social stratification**. Martha's Vineyard is a small island off the coast of New England, popular with summer visitors. The two phonetic variables Labov selected were (**ay**) and (**aw**); (ay) as in *while, pie* pronounced as /ai/ or /ei/ and (aw) as in *out, house* pronounced as /au/ or /eu/.

The preferred pronunciations of most local residents, regardless of social class, were the (*ay*) and (*aw*) sounds used by the local Martha's Vineyard fishermen. This was despite the fact that many people in non-manual occupations (especially in the 31–45 age group) had only returned after extensive periods working or at college on the mainland. In view of people's tendency to prefer prestige norms, they might have been *expected* to prefer the standard pronunciations of the summer visitors. But they didn't. Labov concluded that these Martha's Vineyard residents deliberately adopted local pronunciation to differentiate themselves from summer visitors, thus expressing **language loyalty** and **solidarity** with other native Vineyarders.

The table below shows the attitudes of three groups of residents to Martha's Vineyard, ranging from *positive* and *neutral* to *negative*. There is a striking correlation between the use of (*ay*) and (*aw*) pronunciation and the subjects' *positive* feelings about the island.

Degree of centralization of (ay) and (aw) by age level on Martha's Vineyard

Age	(ay)	(aw)
75–	25	22
61–75	35	37
46–60	62	44
31–45	81	88
14–30	37	46

Source: Labov (1972)

1 Look at the diagram on page 18. What do you notice about the differences in age and pronunciation?

2 This is your opportunity to undertake some sociolinguistic research! Choose a local *phonological variable* (ie a distinctive feature of the regional accent used where you live for example the pronunciation of short /a/ as in *bath* and *grass* contrasts with the RP long /a/ in *baath* and *graass*.

3 Visit three selected shops or department stores in your local town or city, roughly comparable to Saks, Macy's and S. Klein in their clienteles.

■ Decide on *one question* to ask in three departments of each store. The question must elicit your chosen phonological variable in people's answers *at least once*.

■ Alternatively decide on three *different questions* to ask in *each* shop. Again, each question must elicit the phonological variable at least once.

■ Note down whether the respondents use the regional pronunciation or RP.

■ Tabulate your findings in the same way as the Labov diagram on page 18.

■ Are they comparable with Labov's findings, linking prestige pronunciation with the more expensive shop or store?

Peter Trudgill

Peter Trudgill is a British sociolinguist who has worked on linguistic variables, social class and English regional dialects. His research in Norwich focused on *phonological* and *grammatical variables* in relation to social class. We shall look at two of his studies, one on phonological variables, one on grammatical variables.

Norwich, 1974: phonological variables

Trudgill studied the use of three *phonological* or *pronunciation variables* in Norwich:

■ /ng/ as in (*singin'*: RP *singing*)
■ /t/ as in (*bo'l*: RP *bottle*)
■ /h/ as in (*eart*: RP *heart*)

When he analysed his data, Trudgill divided his subjects (people he had recorded in Norwich) into five social classes:

1 LWC (lower working class)
2 MWC (middle working class)
3 UWC (upper working class)
4 LMC (lower middle class)
5 MMC (middle middle class).

Trudgill took note of two other important factors: he noted the *gender* of his subjects (which will be referred to again in Chapter 4); and he noted the *differences* between *careful* and *casual* speech (ie *careful* – formal style [FS]; reading of word lists [WLS]; reading passage style [RPS]; *casual* – [CS] informal conversation). He wanted to see if either *gender* or *careful casual* speech affected people's use of *phonological variables*.

His findings showed that:

- the *lower* the social class, the more frequent the *regional* pronunciation
- *women* tended to prefer RP to regional pronunciation (preference for prestige forms because of linguistic insecurity)
- in *casual* speech MMC men used the regional form [*singin*] (possibly due to the more 'macho' connotations); in *careful* speech they preferred RP [*singing*].

These findings suggest that use of the *phonological variable* /ng/ in Norwich is affected by *social class, gender* and *social context*.

Norwich, 1974: grammatical variables

Trudgill also investigated the use of *grammatical variables* in the context of social class. The one he chose was the (-s) marker used in third person singular present tense verbs (ie *he sings, she dances*). This grammatical variable is always used in Standard English, but is often omitted in regional varieties (eg *he dance, she sing*).

Trudgill found that *social class* directly affected usage of (-s):

- 97% of LWC subjects omitted (-s)
- 29% of LMC subjects omitted (-s)
- 0% of UMC subjects omitted (-s)

Another study of Black American English speakers in Detroit (**Wolfram**, 1974) produced similar (though less dramatic) results. Below is a comparison of Trudgill's and Wolfram's findings about the use of the grammatical variable [-s]:

Class	Trudgill (Norwich)	Wolfram (Detroit)
UMC	0%	1%
LMC	29%	10%
UWC	75%	57%
MWC	81%	(no figure provided)
LWC	97%	71%

Clearly Trudgill's research has pioneered new approaches to the study of language and social class in Britain.

Petyt (1977) and Macaulay (1977, 1991)

Like Trudgill, Petyt also studied use of the *phonological variable* (h) as in *eart*, but in the West Riding of Yorkshire. He found that his Bradford subjects omitted [h] at the beginning of a word much more frequently than the Norwich subjects.

Class	Trudgill (Norwich)	Petyt (Bradford)
MMC	6%	12%
LMC	14%	28%
UWC	40%	67%
MWC	60%	89%
LWC	60%	93%

Petyt concluded that omission of [h] was a major characteristic of West Yorkshire speech, but a minor characteristic of Norwich speech. Again, social class was a significant factor in usage.

Like Trudgill, Macaulay investigated the omission of the *phonological variable* (t), known as the **glottal stop** (*bo'l*), in Glasgow. He also found a direct correlation between *social class* and the *glottal stop*: it was used by 68.8% of LWC speakers and by 0% of UMC and MMC speakers.

Lesley and James Milroy (1978, 1980, 1987)

The Milroys (separately and together) have also researched *linguistic variables* in relation to *social class*, taking a different perspective, and using different ways of collecting evidence. First, they studied the language of a *single social class* (working-class communities in Belfast). Secondly, they paid particular attention to the *gender* of their subjects. Thirdly, they placed their informants in the context of their *social networks* (look back to p.4 to remind yourself of the definition). Their aim was to investigate the role of *casual speech* within three Belfast communities:

1 Ballymacarrett (Protestant, low male unemployment)
2 The Hammer (Protestant, substantial male unemployment)
3 The Clonard (Catholic, substantial male unemployment).

They found that:

■ the stronger the *social network*, the greater the use of *vernacular* or *non-standard* linguistic features (remember that *vernacular* means everyday, informal, non-standard, spoken language)
■ in Protestant Ballymacarrett and the Hammer, women used *fewer* vernacular features than men and preferred *prestige forms* (as Trudgill found in Norwich)
■ in Catholic Clonard, however, younger women preferred *non-prestige forms*, contrary to the conventional practice of Ballymacarrett and the Hammer, as a way of showing *social solidarity* with their unemployed men.

These findings demonstrate the importance of *social networks* within a *social class* and their influence on the way people use language in their *speech communities*. They also show that apparent norms, like women's well-documented preference for prestige forms (*hypercorrection*), can be reversed (consciously or otherwise) by the need to express something more important (ie *social solidarity*).

Jenny Cheshire (1982)

Like the Milroys, Cheshire focused her research on a *single social class* (working-class teenagers in Reading) and their use of non-standard English *grammatical* variables. These included:

- lack of agreement between subject and verb ('*we **goes** shopping*', '*we **has** a little fire*', '*you **was** outside*')
- the use of double negative ('*I'm **not** going **nowhere***', '*I **never** done **nothing***')
- using '*what*' (pronoun used in *questions*) as a substitute for the relative pronoun '*that*' ('*there's a knob **what** you turn*')
- use of present for past tense ('*I **come** down here yesterday*').

She constructed what she called a **vernacular index**. Cheshire's *vernacular index* was a set of criteria for assessing her subjects' use of non-standard vernacular forms. The *vernacular index* for boys' usage related to their ambition, degree of 'toughness' and peer group status. The *vernacular index* for girls' usage related to more personal factors, including preference for prestige forms. Cheshire's conclusions were that:

- boys used non-standard vernacular forms according to culture and peer group
- girls showed much less consistent patterns of vernacular loyalty.

Kevin McCafferty (1995, 1999)

McCafferty studied a Northern Ireland *speech community* in Londonderry (different from the urban Belfast community investigated by the Milroys). He focused on the effects of three social factors on the use of certain phonological variables: *class*, *age* and *ethnicity* (not the usual meaning of 'ethnicity', but in Northern Ireland *religious* difference between Protestant and Catholic has come to mean *racial* difference). It's also important to realise that NIE (Northern Irish English) is the equivalent of SE (Standard English). So Londonderry usage is a 'regional' variation, just like Norwich or Bradford usage.

McCafferty expected that MC (Middle Class) informants would use NIE standard forms and WC (Working Class) informants would prefer Londonderry English non-standard forms, but his findings were a little different:

- Catholics *and* Protestants (regardless of social class) preferred NIE (standard or regional versions) to Southern Irish or RP forms.
- MC and WC *Catholics* preferred Londonderry English non-standard forms.
- MC *Protestants* were more likely to use NIE standard forms.

McCafferty concluded that *social class* did affect speakers' choice of NIE standard or Londonderry English non-standard forms, but it was *less significant than religious ethnicity*.

ACTIVITY 12

Soap operas on radio and television attempt to provide a convincing portrayal of contemporary British society. Your task is to video or tape an episode of the soap opera of your choice. Then listen to the dialogue carefully two or three times before answering the following questions. (You should use your tape-recording or video to provide examples.)

*Remember that the actors are all playing a part and may not normally speak like this. Watch out too for **social** stereotyping!*

1   Is it possible to recognise differences in social class between characters in the episode you selected? Choose *three* different 'characters' to study in detail.

2   Write down as many language features as possible for each character to establish their *idiolect* and *social class.*

3   Is there non-linguistic evidence to support your categorisation of the characters that you selected?

4   Can you find any evidence which links use of *prestige* forms with gender?

5   Compare your findings in small or large group discussion.

NB Don't worry about the fact that scripted dialogue rarely uses non-fluency features, and so is not strictly 'true to life'. In all other respects (lexis, accent, grammar, syntax, standard and non-standard usage) the script will be realistic.

ACTIVITY 13

Here are some suggestions for a range of activities and investigations in the field of language and social class.

You may find it interesting to consider linguistic social stereotyping in *non-British soaps* (i.e. American or Australian) *or* in British films of the 1940s and 1950s. Similarly, there is scope for investigations in:

- girls' and boys' school stories from earlier in the twentieth century (e.g. Angela Brazil, Elinor Brent-Dyer, Enid Blyton [girls']; or 'Molesworth' [boys']); or more recently the Harry Potter books
- diaries such as *The Secret Diary of Adrian Mole aged 13¾, The Diary of a Nobody* or *Bridget Jones's Diary*
- advertisements from the past (in newspapers or women's magazines)
- comics and newspapers from earlier in the twentieth century (*News Chronicle, Manchester Guardian, Schoolfriend, Boys' Own Paper*)

The purpose of these tasks is to set you thinking about issues of language and social class in an accessible way. Remember that *social stereotypes,* linguistic or non-linguistic, always need to be examined critically.

Dialect and accent

What do we mean by 'dialect'?

Dialect means the specific *vocabulary, syntax* (or sentence structure) and *grammar* of **one particular variety of English**, including the way its speakers *pronounce* it. You can have **regional** (including *rural* and *urban*) *dialects,* as well as *social dialects.*

This can be a confusing area, because people think that the terms **accent** and **dialect** are interchangeable. They're not! *Accent* means pronunciation *only*. You need to make sure that you are quite clear about the difference. *Dialect* is a much broader term, including *all* the language systems.

A **British regional dialect** is quite simply the variety of English spoken in a particular *region* of the UK. The most extreme forms could be described as *rural dialects*. These tend to be spoken by older people living in geographically isolated areas. Most of us find it easier to recognise regional *accents* than regional *dialects*. We're vaguely aware that some *grammatical* usage 'isn't standard English', or that a word 'sounds local'; we'd certainly be hard pressed to describe the grammar and vocabulary of our own local dialect. This is because most of the English we hear in the media or in education is the *dialect* or *variety* of English called **Standard English**.

Written regional dialect (e.g. in stories, poems, newspaper articles) does exist, but it tends to be of interest only to local people, tourists, or students of dialect (**dialectologists**). Regional dialects date back to the times when communications were poor, and language change was much slower. The powerful influence of the media, together with urbanisation and increased social mobility, means that much regional dialect has been lost. People even confuse dialect with slang! However, it's important that language history should not be wiped out entirely, and dialect enthusiasts (and perhaps A level English Language students) have their contribution to make in protecting these regional dialects.

Urban dialects are recent growth areas, though they derive from earlier regional and rural dialects. We shall be looking at these in more detail shortly. What is interesting is that an *urban dialect* in an industrial area like Greater Manchester simultaneously includes: the *Southern glottal stop* (*bo'l* for 'bottle'); the *Northern* short vowel /a/ (*bath* not *baath*); the *Lancashire* vowel /u:/ (*boook* not *buk*); and the *fossilised pronoun* from *Middle English* (*oo* for *she*, as in 'oo went home late last night'). So *urban dialects* can blend the old with the new, sharing similarities *across* the regions, as well as keeping local differences.

Social dialects in English today include *Standard English (SE)*, *Scottish Standard English* and *Northern Irish English* (NIE). Originally regional varieties, they are now the prestige standard forms in England, Scotland and Northern Ireland. *Standard English* was the dialect used in the South East, selected by Caxton when he printed the first book in English in 1473. It has been the prestige *written* form of English since then, and over time has become the preferred *spoken* usage of educated people (pronounced with an RP or a regional accent). SE is also the variety used in education, the government, the media, and the public domain in general. Scottish SE and NIE differ slightly from SE but basically perform the same function.

ACTIVITY 14

1 What dialect *vocabulary* is used in your local area for the following objects, locations or physical features? How many different versions of the following words can you collect from people you know? Try to match the following words with the dialect words in italics (some of the words have several dialect versions).

stream; money; snail; feeling the cold; a narrow path or way between houses; hungry; marbles; to spin round; soft shoes (for PE); mist; dandelion; toffee; flea; very busy; door latch; show-off; underwear; term of address; autumn; bad-smelling; to creak; bread rolls; tiny piece of wood under the skin; left-handed; to play; squint; spoilt; to go; truce (children's game); gooseberry; mid-morning drink or snack; ghost; go shopping

daps; *smooting*; *wynde*; *spell*; *cuddy-wifted*; *drong*; *lonning*; *dolly-pawed*; *earwig*; *sneck*; *hen*; *cob*; *tuffy*; *mardy*; *snap*; *drinkings*; *butty*; *nudger*; *jigger*; *ollies*; *segs*; *taws*; *backend*; *barley*; *queens*; *beck*; *goosegog*; *laik*; *lop*; *manky*; *nesh*; *barghast*; *do the messages*; *boggart*; *ginnel*; *snobs*; *swank-pot*; *throng*; *mizzle*; *dodman*; *dindle*; *dag*; *bor*; *loke*; *frit*; *gorp*; *erriwiggle*; *dissables*; *cruckle*; *cag-handed*; *smur*; *twizzle*; *peamix*; *clammed*; *to gan*

2 Listen to people talking on the bus, in the supermarket, in the doctors' waiting room etc in the course of a week, and jot down any dialect *grammatical* forms you hear (eg '*that were good*'; '*tha's etten well*'; '*we was on the way home, but missed bus*'; '*I dassent*' [dare not]; '*I ewe him ten quid*'; '*he worked while six last night*'). Sort your findings according to the *frequency* of occurrence, and compare your results with other people's.

3 Compile a dialect dictionary for your area (it doesn't have to be enormous!).

Dialect history

The history of dialects is also the history of the English language. In 1873 the English Dialect Society was founded by W. W. Skeat to further the scientific study of dialect. In the twentieth century, the Survey of English Dialects (University of Leeds) and the Linguistic Survey of Scotland (University of Edinburgh) continued Skeat's work. You can look up your local dialect in the *Linguistic Atlas of England* (1978) or in *Word Maps* (1987). Recently there have been important changes in **dialectology** (the study of dialects). Because of urbanisation and social mobility, *rural* dialects are spoken less and *urban* dialects are emerging as new areas for research. Even so, real differences remain between the North, the Midlands and the South in quite ordinary everyday language. For example, the Old English word *folk* is still used in the Midlands and North, whilst the French word *people* dominates in the South. People who sew use a *bobbin* (French) in the North, whilst people in the South and West prefer *reel* (German) or *spool* (Old Norse). Another North–South difference – do you *lay* the table or *set* it? Most people in the West and South *lay* it, most people from East Anglia to Northumberland *set* it!

What you need to know about dialect today is that although much local *vocabulary* has been lost, **historical grammatical forms** (double negative 'I didn't do nothing' and plural subject, singular verb 'we was late for school') **are still being used** throughout the country. However, because it is not SE usage, people's *attitude* to dialect grammar tends to be *negative*, and these historical forms are *stigmatised*.

Collecting local dialect terms (especially from older speakers) is a good way of discovering what is going on in your area linguistically. In many regions there are publications available (often humorous) giving written versions of local dialect, like *Larn Yourself Norfolk*, *Derbyshire Drawl*, *Learn Yerself Scouse*, *Yorkshire English*, or '*Owd Yer Tight* (Nottingham). Studying local *place-names* provides other insights into local dialect as well as telling you about local history. The English Place-Name Survey is based at the University of Nottingham, and continues to research and collate place-names in England. Place-names provide fascinating – and surprising – research material. (You might like to look up your local place-names – see Further Reading for references.)

What do we mean by 'accent'?

Quite simply, it means the way we *pronounce* the language we speak every day. Accents can also be *regional* or *social*.

Regional accents can be described in **generalised** terms: 'He's got a Northern accent', 'Her accent's Southern, I think', 'You can tell they're Scottish', 'He's from Ireland – listen to him!', 'Her accent's certainly Welsh', or as a **specifically local** accent: 'You can tell she was born in Belper, not Derby!'

Located within the group of *regional accents* are **urban accents** (e.g. London, Birmingham, Manchester, Liverpool, Newcastle, Glasgow); **county** or **rural accents** like Lancashire, Yorkshire, Somerset, Devon, Norfolk; and other **semi-regional accents** like 'Scouse' (Merseyside), Black Country, 'Geordie', Cockney.

Social accents are the accents adopted by a social group which has **no regional base**. *Received Pronunciation (RP)* remains the principal *social accent* today (though some linguists would call *Estuary English*, a recently developed South Eastern accent, a social accent too). RP notably gives no indication of someone's regional origins (though historically it actually originated in the South East). According to the New Zealand sociolinguist Janet Holmes (*Introduction to Sociolinguistics*, 1992) it is 'the accent of the best educated and most prestigious members of English society'. Only a very small percentage of the population of the UK speaks 'pure' RP (though older members of the Royal family speak *exaggerated* RP). Most RP speakers today use a *modified* or *mainstream* version, which may even have faint regional undertones. The diagram below demonstrates RP usage neatly, showing RP (most prestigious) at the apex of the triangle, regional variation at the base, and 'social variation' (ie social class and status) as the variable side of the triangle.

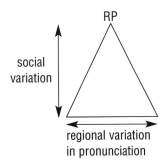

From p.6 of Hughes and Trudgill, *English Accents and Dialects* (London: Arnold, 1979)

Why is it important to know about dialect and accent?

People have surprisingly strong views about their own and other people's pronunciation and non-standard usage, as we saw earlier (p.8–9). They may feel mildly interested and affectionate about local dialect terms, but the real issues associated with accent and dialect are to do with *social class* and *social stereotyping*.

ACTIVITY 15

1 Make two lists, one of the regional accents you *like*, and the other of accents you *dislike*, giving brief reasons for your choices. Compare lists within your group.
2 List the *regional* and *social accents* heard in the course of a single day on radio and/or television in one of the following areas: news-reporting; advertising; sitcoms and soaps; weather forecasting. In your chosen category, note which accents were used most frequently, and suggest reasons.

These tasks should give you some first-hand experience of investigating local and national variations in dialect and accent. You may be interested in finding out more about your regional dialect/accent – the local library should be able to help you. Important **research issues** in the field of *accent and dialect* are listed below, some of which we shall be looking at briefly.

- the history of individual regional dialects, together with the influences affecting their development
- the social implications of positive and negative attitudes to social and regional accents (eg *matched guise* experiments)
- the growth of new urban accents and dialects, such as *Estuary English* and other urban dialects
- dialect levelling (how differences between dialects are being 'smoothed out')
- the influence of young people on dialect and accent change.

Attitudes to dialect and accent

It's useful first to distinguish between **regional** and **social attitudes** to accent and dialect. Activity 15 gave you the opportunity to work out your own views about a range of accents. How you feel about your own local accent may be different from your attitude to *other* regional accents (it may well be a love–hate relationship!). This kind of judgement tends to be *subjective* and reflect regional loyalty. However, if your own attitudes have been influenced by media representations of regional accents, or by the attitudes of people in authority (teachers, employers etc), your judgement may be *social* rather than *personal.*

You may also be affected by certain public **social stereotypes** (e.g. 'Northerners drink beer and are thick', 'Southerners are feeble and think themselves posh'). Most of us recognise the absurdity of these judgements, but many similarly absurd accent and dialect stereotypes are regularly exploited by the advertising industry. Television advertising seems especially susceptible to *linguistic stereotyping*; for example, West Country accents are linked with dairy products, Northern accents with beer and 'traditional' baked bread, and Received Pronunciation with expensive beauty products and financial services. Presumably, these accent stereotypes are meant to make a product even more appealing. *Regional dialect* is occasionally used for similar purposes, but only in the same region, or with a 'translation' provided for a national audience.

Changing stereotypes, however, according to *Times* journalist John Morrish, mean that accent associations can change too: he considers that 'Scouse' no longer signifies 'wit and charm' but 'fecklessness', 'Brum' sounds 'miserable', Cockney sounds 'devious and aggressive' and West Country speakers sound like 'simpletons'.

Attitudes to the use of regional dialect vary, as we saw earlier, partly because boundaries between *regional dialects* and *non-standard English* have been blurred. Not so in Germany, where a recent news item provoked a heated debate about the validity of regional dialects (*Guardian*, 21 October 1999). A nine year old's school report attributed his academic problems to the fact that he spoke the local Bavarian dialect, and not High German (standard educated usage). Public debate about the *status* of regional dialects in Germany and German-speaking Switzerland raged furiously. Could this kind of public argument happen here?

ACTIVITY 16

The purpose of this exercise is to study the use of *accent stereotyping* in television advertising. This will be linked with intended audience, television channel and time of day. Select any commercial television channel and choose *either* a week-day (Monday to Thursday) *or* a week-end day (Friday to Sunday). Look at about 10 'commercial breaks' and:

■ identify the expected audience (look at the programmes on either side of the commercial break as well as the channel)
■ list the products
■ identify the accents used for each product
■ suggest reasons for the choice of accent
■ look for connections between accent, product and audience.

Compare your findings with other people's in your group.

Dialect and accent research studies

Research studies in accent started in 1967, with **W. Lambert's** first *matched guise* experiment to assess people's attitudes to accent. He was studying attitudes to Québec French among French- and English-speaking Canadians. **H. Giles and P. Powesland** adopted Lambert's methods in their study of *attitudes to accent* in the UK, described below.

Matched guise experiment, 1975

A researcher, equally at home speaking with an RP or Birmingham accent, gave an identical talk to *two different groups* of 17-year-old students, introducing himself as a university lecturer. With one group he adopted the *guise* of an RP accent; with the other he adopted the *guise* of a Birmingham accent. Later the students were asked to write down their views about the researcher's 'suitability as a university lecturer'. The student group who heard him using RP preferred him as a lecturer in his RP *guise*; the other group thought him less suitable as a lecturer using a Birmingham accent. The only possible explanation for these responses was the students' *prejudice* in *favour* of RP and *against* a Birmingham accent.

Other accent studies have invited people to rate speakers using *different accents* on a scale of personal qualities (honesty, friendliness, intelligence, self-confidence, sense of humour, ambition, sincerity), or to match supposed occupations to accents of recorded speakers (Is this a doctor, teacher, football player, construction worker?) The results have shown similar *prejudices* to those revealed in Giles and Powesland's matched guise experiment.

ACTIVITY 17

List all the accents you know (including RP) down one side of A4 paper. Divide your sheet into columns representing a range of age and gender (e.g. child, teenager, parent, older sister, neighbour, grandparent, family friend, teacher etc). Include a column for yourself. Use the code L (like), D (dislike) and N (neutral) and *invite responses*. When you have completed the table, write a brief commentary on your findings, and offer any explanations you can.

You may like to compare your findings with those of **John Honey** in *Does Accent Matter?* (1989) where he comments that the majority of people 'rate RP as the most favoured accent, on such criteria as communicative effectiveness, social status and . . . pleasantness of sound'. According to Honey, educated Scottish, Welsh and Irish accents rate next, followed by 'a broad cluster of English provincial accents', including Northern (especially Yorkshire), West Country and Geordie, with Cockney, Scouse, Glaswegian and West Midlands and Birmingham at the bottom of the scale.

What reasons do people offer for their opinions?

Honey considers that *social stereotyping*, rather than the way accents *sound*, is the explanation. People *say* they like the way RP sounds 'correct, clear, beautiful', but *really* they like its prestige *class* associations. Other research suggests (more negatively) that, although RP speakers are regarded as *competent*, speakers using certain *regional* accents are thought to have more *personal integrity* and *social attractiveness*.

A real life example of this controversy about accents happened quite recently. At the 1999 W.H. Smith Literary Award ceremony, the winner, Liverpool novelist Beryl Bainbridge, declared that 'all children should be forced to have compulsory elocution lessons to erase traces of their regional accents'. Not surprisingly, this led to dramatic headlines in the press, especially as Bainbridge added that she hated the Scouse accent and thought that it and other regional accents should be 'wiped out'! A few days later Bainbridge published her own account, claiming that at the award luncheon 'I was a little too merry ... and offended a great many people – including citizens of my native Liverpool'. She went on to say 'I am not against the accents of the Scotch (*sic*), the Welsh, the Irish and the Lancastrian, for such speech is music to my ears. On the other hand, the mangled language spoken by some citizens of Birmingham and Liverpool is a disgrace ... I am not in favour of talking posh (*sic*), simply in favour of correct grammar and fluency.' What is fascinating about Bainbridge's comments is that she starts with criticism of *accent* and ends up criticising *dialect*!

Other public figures have markedly different attitudes to their own regional accent; the journalist Julie Burchill comments sharply on hostile attitudes to her own South West (Bristol) accent, and adds defiantly:

'I don't think I could ever go home for good, but I can carry my home with my voice ... Yes, I am from the western English working class ... Yes, I love my voice, because it speaks to me ... of someone who is resourceful, unbowed, original and, above all, untamed. Would I swop it for a received pronunciation job, modulated and acceptable and like every other godawful boring journalist's voice? I'd rather have my tongue cut out.'   (Source: *Guardian*, February 2000).

Accommodation theory

Howard Giles (1975, 1991) developed this theory to explain the way people *converge* towards or *diverge* from the speech and accent of the person they are talking with. He suggested that *convergence* expresses *social solidarity* with the other speaker; *divergence* expresses a wish to *increase social distance* from the other speaker. For example, a television interviewer who normally uses RP might modify his or her *prestige* accent to *converge* with an interviewee with a marked regional accent. On the other hand, if the interviewee thoroughly disliked an interviewer, they might deliberately *exaggerate* their regional accent, to *diverge* from RP. You could amuse yourself thinking of pairs of people who might need to accommodate when they met, and who would accommodate to whom (e.g. the Queen and Ali G).

Most of us are aware of this unconscious tendency to 'fit in' accent-wise when we visit another part of the country. Giles suggests that *power* is also involved. In an interaction the person with less power is more likely to *converge* with the more powerful person's speech. *Social context* seems to provide the clearest explanation for either *convergence* or *divergence*.

ACTIVITY 18

You can only do this experiment with the co-operation of a member of your family or a good friend! Place a tape-recorder near your front door so that all the doorstep encounters (over 1 or 2 days) can be recorded (i.e. postman, delivery person, friend, doorstep salesman). The idea is to find out whether the person who opens the door *accommodates* to each new person, and what language features change each time.

NB If this can be done, it would make an excellent language investigation topic.

Codeswitching is another kind of *accommodation strategy* (see p.3). We all do it, often unconsciously, when we adapt spoken language to match a new situation and new participants in an interaction. *Codeswitching* can take place in many contexts: people switch *register* (eg from informal to formal); they change from *standard* to *non-standard usage*; or from *one language to another* (e.g. bilingual speakers of Punjabi and English, or Canadian French and English); or *between several languages* (French, Dutch and Flemish are all 'official languages' in Belgium).

Urban accents and dialects

With increasing urbanisation, better communications, the rise of social mobility and the power of the media, there have been new developments in *urban accents* and *dialects*, including so-called *Estuary English*, and the *dialect levelling* seen in major cities and urban areas throughout the UK.

Estuary English

This is a term which was first used in an article in the *Times Educational Supplement* in October 1984. 'Estuary' meant the Thames Estuary. Since then it has been used more and more frequently to describe a new *pronunciation* of Standard English, half-way between London regional and RP. David Crystal describes *Estuary English* as representing the 'confluence of two social trends; an up-market movement of originally Cockney speakers, and a down-market trend towards "ordinary" (as opposed to "posh" speech) by the middle class'.

The gradual spread of Estuary English from the South East across the country has been continuous, helped by the fact that public figures like Ben Elton, Jonathan Ross, Joanna Lumley, and Ken Livingstone, as well as various pop culture icons are said to use it. London-influenced pronunciation changes have been noted by researchers in other urban 'estuary' areas like Chester (the Dee), Liverpool (the Mersey), Hull (the Humber) and Bristol (the Severn) – they are all readily accessible to the capital via the motorway systems.

Common *pronunciation* features of *Estuary English* are:

- *glottalisation* – the glottal stop replaces /t/ before consonants and at the end of a word (Ga' wick airpor'; le'er; se'off (*set off*); qui' ri' (*quite right*); sea'bel' (*seat belt*))
- the replacement of final /l/ by a /u/ vowel (*mill* becomes /miu/; *fulfil* becomes /fulfiu/). A *Sunday Times* article (14 March 1993) suggests the Estuary English version of the RP/SE 'What a delightful meal this lunch

was, thank you' would be 'Wha' an absolu'ee deligh'fuw meaw this lunch was, cheers'.

Characteristic *grammatical* features of *Estuary English* include:

- the use of *never* (as in 'I never did. No, I never')
- the 'confrontational' question tag ('I said I was going, didn't I?').

Even the lexis of Estuary English reflects change – for example, '*thank you*' has become '*cheers*'.

The effects of *Estuary English* pronunciation on traditionalist pressure groups like The Queen's English Society are predictable: 'God forbid that it becomes standard English. Are standards not meant to be upheld? We must not slip into slovenliness because of a lack of respect for the language' as one commentator declared.

Dialect levelling

The new town of Milton Keynes was established in 1969 to house a population overspill of Londoners in rural Buckinghamshire. It is now a city, having expanded dramatically over the last three decades of the twentieth century. 65% of the population came from the South East of England and 40% from London. Milton Keynes has been the location of a linguistic research project undertaken by **P. Kerswill and A. Williams** (1994) to discover whether a new *urban dialect* has developed there. They chose to focus on the speech of *children* to look for possible evidence of a new dialect (rather than adults with established pronunciation and language usage). They found that the children's speech *differed* significantly, both from the speech of their parents and carers *and* from the speech of older local residents.

Kerswill and Williams found that similar changes are taking place in Reading (90 km south) and Cambridge (80 km east), and spreading north to other urban centres, again with *young people* leading the changes. They suggest that **dialect** and **accent levelling** are taking place across the South East and elsewhere in the country, but still remain confident that *regional differences* in accent and dialect will not be lost. Kerswill and Williams's findings have been confirmed by other researchers investigating the language of young people in Hull and Reading (Kerswill and Williams, 1998), in Newcastle (Watt and Milroy, 1999) in Derby (Foulkes and Docherty, 1999) and the Sheffield dialect of older rural males (Stoddart, Upton and Widdowson, 1999).

The conclusion seems to be that there is a *generalised* movement in accents towards a kind of national, rather than regional pronunciation, as a result of *levelling*, rather than *standardisation*. This movement in accents has its origins in London working-class speech, and is spread by young people.

Regional accents, however, do still have an important role to fulfil. Perhaps surprisingly, they are highly valued by companies with *call centres* (i.e. large offices where businesses like insurance and banking are run via the telephone networks). These companies deliberately locate their call centres in areas where the *local* accent rates highly on the national scale – places like the North East, southern Scotland, and Derby – in order to create a good impression on their customers!

ACTIVITY 19

Do you use *Estuary English*? Has your accent been *levelled*? Record yourself talking informally with friends, and then listen for the following pronunciation features:

- *glottal stop*
- /iw/ instead of -ll or -l at the end of a word
- /f/ or /v/ instead of /th/

- the vowel sound /ou/ as in *coat*.

Compare your findings with other people's in the group (keep a tally if possible), and add up the results of everyone in the class/group. Do the findings in your group *confirm* that accent and dialect levelling is taking place in your area?

Standard and non-standard English

We have been referring to *standard* and *non-standard usage* in the course of this chapter as if the concept of *standardisation* had already been discussed. The **Standard English** we use today has its origins in the South East, based on the East Midlands dialect of Middle English chosen by William Caxton in 1473 for his first printed book. Because the South East was a centre of wealth and population, and included the universities of Oxford and Cambridge, its *regional* dialect became a *social* dialect, with all the prestige and status that economic and social power can give.

A

DICTIONARY

OF THE

ENGLISH LANGAUGE

IN WHICH

The WORDS are deduced from their ORIGINALS,

AND

ILLUSTRATED in their DIFFERENT SIGNIFICATIONS

BY

EXAMPLES from the best WRITERS

TO WHICH ARE PREFIXED

A HISTORY of the LANGUAGE,

AND

AN ENGLISH GRAMMAR.

BY SAMUEL JOHNSON, A.M.

IN TWO VOLUMES

VOL. I

LONDON

Printed by W. Stranan

For J. and P. KNAPTON; T. and T. LONGMAN; C. HITCH and L. HAWES;

A. MILLAR; and R. and J. DODLEY

MDCCLV

Samuel Johnson, *A Dictionary of the English Language* (1755)

Samuel Johnson

Standardising written language means that everyone who is literate, wherever they live, can understand it. However, as Romaine points out (p. 84) 'standardisation is also one of the main agents of inequality', because the illiterate or poorly educated are even more disempowered. Hence those who use non-standard forms are viewed *negatively*, because they are linked with lack of power and status in society.

How the process of standardisation takes place

This description is based on D. Graddol and D. Leith's account of the process of standardisation in *English: history, diversity and change*, (1996 p.139).

1 Selection One dialect or variety is chosen from those available, usually a variety linked with the most *powerful* social group. (Caxton chose the East Midlands dialect rather than West Midlands, Kentish, West Saxon or Northumbrian dialects when he translated from French and produced the first printed book in English.)

2 Codification This means establishing the *norms* of grammar, syntax, spelling, meanings so that everyone uses the same written forms. Later, norms of spoken language are also established. **Dictionaries** and **grammar books** are the best way to achieve codification. *Dictionaries* are particularly crucial: the earliest English dictionaries include *The Dictionarie of Sir Thomas Elyot* (1538) and Samuel Johnson's *A Dictionary of the English Language* (1755). *Grammar books* are also important in the codification process; an important early one is Robert Lowth's *Short Introduction to English Grammar* (1762).

3 Elaboration This process means the development and extension of the resources of a language to increase its functions. For example, the huge influx of Latin, French and Italian words into English in the sixteenth century developed its richness and flexibility; similarly from the seventeenth century the rise of colonialism added many words to English from the indigenous languages of the American and Indian sub-continents.

4 Implementation Standardisation is implemented when printed texts become available in the standard form, ranging from national newspapers to translations of the *Bible*. This *discourages* variation, and *encourages* loyalty to the standard form, as we see today in an organisation like The Queen's English Society which exists to 'preserve the standard' and resist change.

ACTIVITY 20

The time of greatest 'elaboration' of English is hard to identify, but it is an ongoing process. Look up the following words in a good dictionary (*OED* or *Shorter Oxford Dictionary* or *Chambers Dictionary*) and find out the country of origin and date of first usage of the following:

tobacco; *peninsula*; *rhythm*; *theory*; *imitate*; *influence*; *barbecue*; *pyjamas*; *potato*; *tomato*; *editor*; *cushy*; *bungalow*; *restaurant*; *limousine*; *alligator*; *siesta*; *mustang*; *umbrella*; *cookie*; *gin*; *alcohol*; *lemon*; *shampoo*; *tattoo*; *voodoo*; *jazz*

The process of standardisation described above can have negative as well as positive effects; it can lead to *inflexibility* in spoken and written forms, and encourage prejudiced *attitudes* to develop towards any variation from the standard. But there have always been people who grumble about the 'erosion of standards' in English! Linguists call this the **complaint tradition**, and we shall look at it briefly.

The complaint tradition

The complaint tradition has a long history; people have always complained about the terrible state of the language and looked back with nostalgia to the supposed golden age (usually their own youth!) when grammar, syntax, pronunciation and vocabulary were just about perfect. For example . . .

- In 1473 Caxton **complained** about the difficulty in choosing the right dialect for the first printed book in English (there were too many to choose from).
- Sixteenth-century scholars and courtiers **complained** about the loan words from Latin, Greek, Italian and French flooding in and corrupting the 'purity' of English ('terrible windy words' like *inflate, strenuous, reciprocal, emphasis, antipathy*).
- In 1712 Jonathan Swift **complained** in his *Proposal for Correcting, Improving and Ascertaining the English Tongue* that

    '. . . our Language is extremely imperfect; that its daily Improvements are by no means in proportion to its daily Corruptions; that the Pretenders to polish and refine it, have chiefly multiplied Abuses and Absurdities; and, that in many Instances, it offends against every Part of Grammar'.

- People **complain** today about Americanisms, quite unaware that some of these words came from England in the first place.

The *complaint tradition* is often linked with **prescriptivist attitudes** (language must be correct, rules must be followed). Prescriptivists regard language change as a *moral* rather than a linguistic issue, and complain about the 'slovenliness' of spoken language, ignoring the fact that spoken and written English are *different* in structure, lexis and grammar. To *complain* because spoken language does not follow the rules of written language seems illogical and absurd!

Prescriptivism, standardisation and education

There are serious implications here for education. Should teachers only use standard spoken and written English in school? Should they actively discourage non-standard usage under all circumstances? How essential is it to teach the *codified norms* of grammar, syntax and spelling? Recent government policies on improving literacy and implementing the National Curriculum express a clear position. They stress the importance of teaching *Standard English* to all children in both spoken and written forms. Non-standard spoken usage is acceptable in informal contexts, but in formal situations Standard English (with or without regional pronunciation) should be used.

Parents, teachers, school governors (and others with *prescriptivist* attitudes) must recognise that even standardisation is a living, dynamic process and can never be 'set in concrete'.

ACTIVITY 21

Write an article to be published in a school or college magazine or on a suitable website arguing the case for or against the teaching of Standard English in schools.

ACTIVITY 22

1 What aspects of spoken and written English are people *complaining* about today? List as many examples as you can find.

Possible sources of information include letters to the editor (local or national newspapers and magazines), phone-in programmes on radio or television, and press releases of opinions expressed publicly by politicians, Prince Charles, the Queen's English Society, or leading educationalists. Likely areas of complaint include: spelling errors, Americanisms, 'wrong pronunciations', political correctness and taboo language.

2 Ask people you know in the following three age groups (under 25, over 40, over 60) whether they consider the following non-standard usages *acceptable* or *unacceptable*. Keep a tally of their responses, and compare your results.

- That reply is *different from* what I expected.
- We bought some flowers *off* the market stall.
- *Me and Mary* went out last night.
- *Alright*, if you insist.
- Try *and* arrive early.
- They invited my friends and *myself*.
- She doesn't actually dislike computer games – she's just *disinterested* in them.
- It looked *like* it would rain.
- *Hopefully* we will be there in time.
- Everyone must sign *their* exam entry forms.
- He promised to *action* the plan immediately.

Attitudes to English: political correctness

In this chapter we have explored *attitudes to English* in a variety of areas. Our final topic is **political correctness**, the ultimate expression of attitudes (both positive and negative). It concerns the language we use to *avoid discriminating* against people whom we perceive to be *disadvantaged* in our society, because of their *gender, age, race, physical, mental* or *emotional disability*. The English language has always been good at generating **euphemisms** (pleasant ways of saying something unpleasant) for everything from body functions ('go to the bathroom') to drunkenness in celebrities ('tired and emotional') and unpleasant facts like death (to 'pass on' and 'kick the bucket', 'terminate' and 'rub out').

Political correctness attempts to do something much bolder – to compensate (if only slightly) for social inequities, unpleasant stereotypes and unhappy situations by using more positive or at least neutral language to talk about them. This is a tall order!

The problem is that *political correctness* can become as rigid and narrow as the language it attempts to replace. Much journalistic ingenuity has been exercised in mocking PC language, as it avoids 'sexist, racist, speciesist, fattist, lookist or ageist bias' by using terms like *optically challenged* (poor vision), *tonsorially disadvantaged* (bald), *cerebrally challenged* (stupid), or *differently sized* (obese) and the classic *person-hole covers* (manhole covers). In fact, many of these terms have been deliberately invented to discredit the political correctness movement. More serious concerns were raised recently by the Reader's Editor of *The Guardian* in relation to an article by a professor of English literature, in which he referred to disturbed students as 'crazies' and 'nutters' who had 'lost it'. *Mind*, the mental health charity, wrote to *The Guardian* complaining about this offensive and discriminatory way of describing mental health problems. This would seem to be a valid case for political correctness and more imaginative use of language.

What the *political correctness* lobby has achieved is to draw public attention over the last three decades to the way that *language shapes social attitudes*. As a result, some significant changes for the better have taken place. People have learnt that discriminatory language has negative effects, however innocent the intentions of the speaker or writer, and there is a much greater awareness that we really do need to think before we speak! However, the great danger now is less linguistic than political, namely that all attempts to achieve equality and prevent discrimination, are labelled with a sneer by politicians and the press as 'politically correct'. The term has undergone change for the worse, and according to one journalist, has become 'a phrase used to denigrate and contain true liberalism' (Gary Younge, *The Guardian*, February 2000).

ACTIVITY 23

1 Find as many examples as possible of politically correct language in the areas below:

- sex and sexuality
- physical disability
- mental disability
- racial difference.

Your best sources will be: magazines and newspapers (especially broadsheets), radio and television; public information materials (see your local library for leaflets and booklets) and the Internet.

2 Give the Plain English equivalents of the following politically correct terms: *partner; human resources; generously cut; companion; chronologically gifted; economically exploited; birthparent*.

3 What are the arguments for *avoiding* the

following terms: *wheelchair bound*; *cripple*; *chairman*; *authoress*; *negro*; *mistress*; *lunatic*; *spastic*.

4 Write *your own* politically correct story (you may find *Politically Correct Bedtime Stories* a useful model).

Further reading

Cameron, Deborah (1995) *Verbal Hygiene* Routledge

Cameron, Kenneth (1996, revised new edition) *English Place-Names* Batsford

Coulmas, Florian (ed.) (1997) *The Handbook of Sociolinguistics* Blackwell

Crystal, David (1995) *Cambridge Encyclopaedia of the English Language* Cambridge University Press

Foulkes, Paul and Docherty, Gerard (eds.) (1999) *Urban Voices* Arnold

Graddol, David, Leith, Dick and Swann, Joan (1996) *English: history, diversity and change* Open University Press and Routledge

Green, Jonathan (1996) *Chasing the Sun: Dictionary-makers and the dictionaries they made* Pimlico

Milroy, James and Milroy, Lesley (1985) *Authority in Language* Routledge

Romaine, Suzanne (1994) *Language in Society: An Introduction to Sociolinguistics* Oxford University Press

Upton, Clive, Sanderson, Stewart and Widdowson, John (1987) *Word Maps: A Dialect Atlas of England* Croom Helm

Wardhough, Ronald (1986, second edition) *An Introduction to Sociolinguistics* Blackwell

Wilkinson, Jeff (1995) *Introducing Standard English* Penguin

2 English Abroad

In this chapter we shall be looking at the role of English in the world today: different Englishes and their histories; English creoles; learning English as another language; bilingualism and multilingualism. We shall aim to discover *other people's attitudes* towards English throughout the world.

English in the world today – a global language?

How can we estimate the importance and the role of English in the world today? Should the figure be based on the number of mother-tongue speakers, or should we include people for whom English is a second, third or 'official language'? Do we include speakers of English creoles (a language based on English plus another language)? What about international travellers, users of the World Wide Web and global film and television audiences, all of whom need some understanding of English?

Some facts and figures about the English language

The figures below are conservative estimates, based on research from the 1990s. David Crystal thinks that the real total of English speakers in the world (including mother-tongue, fluent and non-fluent speakers) is in excess of 1,000 million (Crystal, 1995, 1997, 1999).

	1995	1999
English as mother tongue (L1 or first language)	427 million	450 million
English as second language (L2)	98 million	150–400 million
English as L2, L3 or L4 (estimated)	300 million	400–600 million
Approximate total 'English speakers' *minimum*	**850 million**	**1.5 billion**

Comparing mother-tongue speakers across the world

Language	Number of speakers
Mandarin Chinese (Beijing-based *standard*)	726 million
English	**427 million**
Spanish	266 million
Hindi, with Urdu	223 million
Arabic	181 million
Russian	158 million
French	116 million

Comparing the total number of speakers

Language	Number of speakers
Mandarin Chinese plus other Chinese language	1,071 million
English	**850 million**
Spanish	350 million
Hindi, with Urdu	350 million
Russian	290 million

Why does everyone want to speak English?

Crystal quotes a Danish university student – 'Nearly everyone in Denmark speaks English. If we didn't, there'd be no-one else to talk to.' UNESCO surveys show that similar attitudes to English prevail everywhere, for the following reasons:

- English is the official or semi-official language in over 60 countries
- it has a prominent place in over 20 other countries, and is a dominant or established language in all six continents
- it is the main language of books, newspapers, airport and air traffic control, international business and scientific conferences, science, technology, medicine, diplomacy, sports, international competitions, pop music and advertising
- 66% of the world's scientists write in English
- 75% of the world's letters are written in English
- 80% of information in the world's electronic retrieval systems is stored in English
- Internet users communicate mostly in English
- 150,000,000 million people listen to radio programmes in English
- more than 130,000,000 children (primary and secondary) study English at school.

ACTIVITY 24

Choose *three* statements from the list above, and *find three pieces of your own evidence* to support each statement (possible sources include libraries, newspapers, the Internet). Share your evidence with other members of your group.

Why has English achieved global status?

Crystal thinks that the chief reasons are the expansion of British colonial power (peaking in the late nineteenth century), and the emergence of the United States as the leading economic power of the twentieth century. Today 'English' means *American English* as well as *English English*, and learners are taught one or the other, depending on the political, economic and cultural climate.

Other languages also have global status (e.g. Arabic, Chinese, French, Russian and Spanish) as well as significant *political* and *economic power*, often based on their colonial past (and present). For example, French colonial expansion in the eighteenth and nineteenth centuries meant that Canada, parts of Africa, Haiti and Martinique are *francophone* (*French-speaking*) countries today. Spanish is spoken throughout South America, apart from Brazil, where the Portuguese were the colonisers. The twentieth century political power of China and Russia means that Chinese and Russian are global languages, as is Arabic in the oil-rich Middle East.

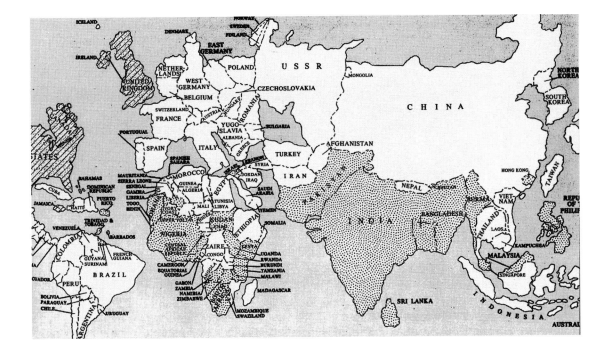

English and the European Union

When the European Union first emerged as an *economic* entity, it was politically crucial that no one language took precedence. English, French and German became the principal languages, with 56, 54 and 78 million native speakers respectively. They top the language hierarchy, with national languages like Dutch, Swedish, Irish and Spanish next, followed by languages like Basque, Scots Gaelic, Welsh, Frisian and Luxembourgish which are 'officially recognised and supported'. Languages like Breton, Cornish, Lallans (Scottish) and Romany (spoken by 'travellers') receive much less support. As political and economic changes take place in the EU, and as new members are added, the language balance may shift somewhat. There will soon be 21 official languages! English, French and Spanish are regarded most favourably for *worldwide* business communication, with German the preferred language for business *within Europe*.

English as a world language – the future?

David Graddol stated (*Redesigning English*, 1996 p.195) that:

'English enjoys a position in the world well beyond that which might be expected by the number of its native speakers. It is undoubtedly at the apex of the complex political, economic and cultural hierarchy of languages in the world.'

Nevertheless, recent projections about world languages suggest that by 2050, with Pacific Rim countries like China, India and Indonesia dominating the world's economy, and with Europe and the Americas losing economic power, **Mandarin Chinese** will be *the* global language everyone will want to learn.

ACTIVITY 25

1 List as many European languages as you can, then find out which *language family* each belongs to (e.g. English is a member of the Germanic language family, which includes Swedish and Norwegian as well as German). Encyclopaedias, the Internet, or reference books (e.g. Katzen, *The Languages of the World*) will provide the information you need. Which language family has the most members?

2 A recent news item (*Guardian*, 10 March 2000) is headed *Interpreters' walk-out leaves Europe's diplomats tongue-tied*. Why they walked out is less important than the 'silencing' of EU diplomats! The news story highlights the crucial importance of interpreters to the successful running of the EU.

Your *task* is to imagine yourself as a native speaker (and potential interpreter) of one of the following languages: Polish, Hungarian, Czech, Estonian or Slovene (all current candidates to join the EU). Prepare a brief statement for a television debate to argue for your language to become an EU official language.

International attitudes to English

International attitudes to English (whether British or American) can vary widely, affected by different social, political, cultural and practical considerations.

Positive attitudes to English abroad are reflected in the endless demand for English classes and the popularity of the influential BBC World Service (radio), together with the ongoing development of *World Standard English*.

Negative attitudes derive from the fact that English has a great deal of influence (some say too much) on other languages worldwide (**language interference**); it can displace smaller languages and even destroy them (**English as** *language killer*).

World Standard English (WSE)

This is currently an idea rather than a reality – one which some people think should remain unrealised. First, how would the differences between the major league players, *British Standard English* and *American Standard English*, be reconciled? Indeed, are they the only Standard Englishes in the world? The diagram below suggests otherwise – and would people want to give up their own version of SE for WSE?

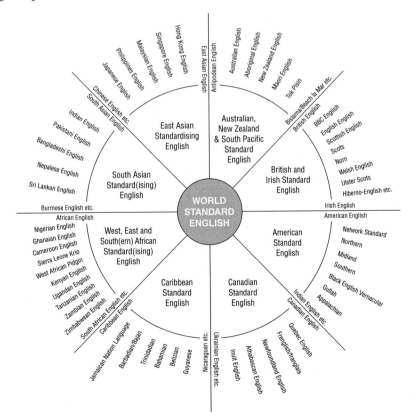

Source: D. Crystal (1995) *The Cambridge Encyclopedia of the English Language,* page 111

Next, would WSE spelling and pronunciation be British or American? . . . Vocabulary choice might become political rather than linguistic – would the American or British world be politically 'better'? The case for World Standard English looks more problematic.

Perhaps a version of WSE will evolve for international business and diplomatic purposes, and for all other purposes individual Standard Englishes will remain separate, developing parallel but uniquely different versions of English.

English and language interference

In view of the global status of English, it is likely to have some influence on other languages. If two languages are being used side by side, some interference between the two is predictable.

An example of **grammatical interference** can be seen among older generation Punjabi/English speakers whose English is still influenced by the grammar of their mother tongue (eg the determiner is omitted in Punjabi '*she bought house in London*').

Vocabulary interference is common, and often unwelcome. France is particularly hostile to English borrowings (*Franglais*) and in the USA Spanish speakers dislike *Spanglish*. Other variants on the same theme are *Singlish* (Singaporean English) and *Polglish* (Polish and English). Recently a law has been passed in Poland forbidding the use of English borrowings without an accompanying translation into Polish.

Franglais (ie *français* and *anglais*) is spoken French which freely *codeswitches* between English and French. These codeswitches may be from either British or American English. Familiar examples are *le weekend, le cocktail, un coke, le drugstore* and more recently (matching social and technological developments) *Eurostar, un baby-boomer, le hamburger, le software, l'airbag*. Rushing to the defence of French (according to *The Times* 12 October 1999) is M. Alfred Gilder, whose book *En Vrai Français* 'attempts to wean the French from their accelerating adoption of American-inspired *franglais*'. Gilder, inspired by the attempts of the *Academie Française* (official guardian of the French language) to halt the tide of change (8000 unwanted Anglicisms), suggests some French alternatives: telecomedie (*le sitcom*); la craque-danse (*le rap*); un moeste (*un must*); messageonique (*un e-mail*); admirette (*un groupie*); hipe (*hip*); pret-a-lire (*bestseller*) etc. Whether these terms will become replacements for *les anglicismes* remains to be seen! Even more worrying for M. Gilder must be the current rise of *verlan* in France (from *l'envers* – reverse or upside down). According to the *Guardian* (27 March 2000), this is a new language fashion among the young, so that *femme* (woman) becomes *meuf*; *flic* (cop) becomes *keuf*; *fete* (party) becomes *teuf*. And he is worrying about Anglicisms!

There are also problems in French-speaking Québec, where the director of linguistic services for *L'Office de la Langue* urged his office colleagues not to use *faxer* as if it were a French verb (*j'ai faxé; tu vas faxer*) but instead to use *telecopier* a message. When using the computer, you must *sauvegarde* (save) your file, but you may *clique* (click) with your *souris* (mouse)!

Spanglish (ie *Spanish* and *English*) has a slightly different history. It derives from the codeswitching of American Hispanics (31 million in the USA) between American English and Spanish. A *Times* report (18 January 2000) describes a new Spanish dictionary as 'peppered with hybrid words' and 'certain to ruffle feathers at the *Real Academia Espagnole* (Royal Spanish Academy)'. This institution is the official guardian of correct (ie Castilian) Spanish, playing a similar role to that of the Academie Francaise in its linguistic conservatism. The sort of Spanglish disapproved of includes terms like *hangyeo* (hanging out); *fri* (free); *guachando el ancorman* (watching the television news anchorman); *yogueando* (jogging); *culismo* (very cool) and *brude* (brother). Ilan Stavans, author of the *Dictionary of Spanglish* has even declared that 'The hispanic world will end up speaking Spanglish!'

Borrowings from English into other languages

It is impossible to estimate the number of words from English absorbed into other languages across the world. This increasing use of Anglicisms and Americanisms results from the rapid development in global communications, and especially the Internet and the World Wide Web. Many governments are less than enthusiastic about this influx, but can do little to prevent it.

ACTIVITY 26

1 Choose a magazine or newspaper article in a modern language you or a friend are reasonably fluent in (French, Spanish, German), and *list* the words borrowed from English (*Anglicisms*). Compare your findings with other people's in the group.

2 The following letter was received by an English academic from a colleague at a French university. Read the letter through carefully. List the errors in the letter, under the headings of vocabulary, spelling and grammar. Do you think his problems with English might be caused by *language interference* between English and French?

Dear Sir J . . .

Just a little note in my very bad English, joined to the letter of our bibliotechary. Please, if you do 'nt disturb, send a facture, to be paid by our university. And forgive me for that trouble. But I am in Paris, totaly in the work of the Agregation of history, and I can't do that facture in your place, for the editorial house. I am very very pleased to have received personaly your Actes, so richful. I had time to read and love them, before my travel and stage to Paris, so I beg them for my department. Many thanks, good holidays, good summer (in Paris, it is beginning awful in the rain and bad weather), and very sincerely I hope to meet you.

K.H.

English – the language killer

This is a drastic view of the role of English as an international language, but it must be considered.

There are approximately 6000 languages in the world today. 5000 are spoken in just 22 countries (eg 850 languages in Papua New Guinea, 670 in Indonesia, 380 in India). ***Just over 80% of the world's languages are spoken by fewer than 5% of the world's population,*** many of whom are small groups of people with little cultural, political or economic power. In these 22 countries the favoured *international* language is English.

Though English may be an official language in the countries where endangered languages exist, it is only an ***indirect*** cause of language death. Languages die because people stop using local tribal languages and prefer *regional* languages (e.g. Bengali or Marathi in India; Hausa, Wolof or Swahili in Africa).

In English-speaking countries like Canada, Australia and the USA, however, English does carry ***direct*** responsibility for the loss of indigenous languages (languages of native peoples). For example, in Australia, over 200 Aboriginal languages have already been lost. This happened suddenly (when children with Aboriginal-speaking parents grew up speaking only English) or gradually (as older speakers began to die out).

We'll take a look at the gradual process of language death (in this case an Australian Aboriginal language) because it represents what happens across the world when another human language dies (Dixon in Goodman Graddol pp. 218–9):

- *Stage 1* Aboriginal language (A) used by full community; although some people know a second language, but all think in A.

- *Stage 2* Some people still have A as their first language (L1), but other people use it as a second language (L2), and prefer English as their first language.

- *Stage 3* Only old people use A as their first language: English has become the dominant language for the community, and people think in English. A is now a simplified L2 with a much reduced vocabulary.

- *Stage 4* Nobody can speak the full original language A. Some people speak a simplified version of A. Younger people speak English with some words from A.

- *Stage 5* Everyone in the community speaks and thinks in English. Any words left from A are made to fit in with English grammar and its rules.

- *A is dead because no one speaks it.*

What is being done about endangered languages?

As we have seen, English bears at least some responsibility for the loss of smaller languages. The linguist David Crystal (*Guardian* 25 October 1999) points out that because the world's languages are disappearing so fast, 'in 100 years time, 3000 will be extinct. We should care about dying languages for the same reason that we care when a species of animal or plant dies … we are talking about intellectual and cultural diversity, not biological diversity, but the issues are the same'.

Crystal's concerns are shared worldwide. The **Foundation for Endangered Languages** (FEL) was established in the UK in 1995; elsewhere, similar groups have been set up by international organisations (UNESCO) and by individual countries (Germany, Japan, USA).

How guilty is English?

As a language of huge international power and influence, English is at the same time a *threat* and an *advantage* to non-native speakers. If learning English in a country is regarded as the best way for people to enhance their job prospects, those who *can't* gain access to English language education are pushed even further down the social ladder. So, indirectly, English exaggerates social inequality. Worse, if many languages are spoken in a country, but English has high prestige, other languages will lose status, with long-term social and cultural consequences.

ACTIVITY 27

Imagine you are a speaker of a language which is threatened with extinction by the increasing spread of English in your country or national group. Working in small groups or pairs, plan a campaign to preserve, encourage and develop people's use of your endangered language. You might want to produce an advertising campaign (television, radio), arrange interviews, produce leaflets, write a speech, or use a medium like drama or even film.

ACTIVITY 28

The BBC World Service broadcasts every day on long wave radio (198 kHz) to a worldwide audience. It has a particularly high reputation for accurate news reporting. Prepare a short talk to be broadcast on the World Service *defending* the globalisation of English.

Different Englishes

How many different Englishes are there? Does the term include Scottish, Welsh and Irish English, as well as American or Australian Englishes? What about Black English (British and American versions)? In this section we shall define what we mean by 'different Englishes', explore the range briefly, focus first on British Englishes and then take a closer look at four selected 'Englishes' abroad (American, Caribbean, Australian and Indian).

To most people in the UK, English is just the language they speak every day, without any sense of it being one of the many 'versions' of English spoken worldwide. Most people are unaware that *Scottish, Welsh* and *Irish English* are just as much 'different Englishes' as American or Indian English. Black English in the UK derives mainly from West Indies **creoles** (see p.59), which in turn derive from a combination of West African languages and English.

The reason that differing versions of English are spoken today as a first language in America, Canada, Australia and New Zealand, and as an 'official' language in India, Africa, and Malaysia has a great deal to do with English colonial history. The sixteenth- and seventeenth-century colonists in America were the first to take the English language abroad, followed in the eighteenth century by the founders of the East India Company, the convicts and free settlers of Australia and the tea and rubber planters of Malaysia (and many others).

As time has passed, changes in vocabulary, pronunciation and even grammar have emerged; today these Englishes differ significantly from the English the early colonists and settlers spoke. We shall have a look at some of these different Englishes shortly. But we shall start first close to home.

British English

There are real differences between *English, Scottish, Welsh* and *Irish English*, which people are vaguely aware of but might not find easy to explain. *English English* remains the dominant variety because it is spoken by the majority of the population of the UK (though using a range of regional, urban and social accents – see Chapter 1). *Scottish, Welsh* and *Irish English* have interesting and rather different histories as neighbours of *English English*.

Scottish English

Scots and *Scottish English* are part of the same continuum, with *Scots* almost a separate language, and *Scottish English* rather nearer to English. The language scene in Scotland today is quite complicated, with marked differences between the pronunciation of the Lowlands, Central Scotland, the North and the North West, and a completely different language, *Scots Gaelic* spoken in the Western Isles and the Northern Isles (where many people are bilingual). *Scots* has been called a northern dialect of English, and like English it was brought over by Germanic and Viking invaders; but many think it is a separate language, because it was spoken for centuries when Scotland was an independent country. With the death of Elizabeth I (1603) the English throne passed to her cousin's son, James I of England and VI of Scotland, and the two countries were ruled as one. *Scots* has remained a unique language (written and spoken) and has its own literary tradition (there is even a translation of the New Testament into Scots). In Scotland you might hear anything from Standard English with a faint Scottish accent to the broadest of Glaswegian dialects. *Scottish English* has many features drawn from *Scots*, as we shall see.

Pronunciation

- vowels: /y/ is added to /u:/ so that *moon* is pronounced as *muin*, *use* as *yuise*, *go* as *gae*; *sore* becomes *sair*; *house* becomes *hoose*; *stone* and *home* become *stane* and *hame*; *take* becomes *tak*; *rise* /ai:/ is different from *rice* /ei/ but *cam* and *calm* are pronounced the same, as are *cot* and *caught*, and *fool* and *full*
- consonants: /l/ is lost at the end of words so that *ball* becomes *baw*, *full* becomes *foo*, *gold* becomes *gowd*, *salt* becomes *saut*; /r/ is rhotic (ie pronounced) in *word, beard, bird, card, cord* etc
- *-ch* as in *loch, nicht* for *night*; in *whale* and *which* the *wh-* is pronounced /hw/.

Grammar

- the negative particle is *nae, no* or *not* as in *Will you no come? It wasnae bad; Will he not listen to you?*
- in *the cat wants out* and *I'll away home* the verb 'to go' is omitted
- *will* is used rather than *shall: Will we be going home soon? Will I answer the phone?*
- pronouns ending with *-self* can be used non-reflexively: *Is himself in? How's yourself today?*
- instead of *aren't I* the tag *amn't I* appears: *I'm late for the party, amn't I?*

Vocabulary

- words like *caddie, collie, golf, scone, glamour* come from Old English, as do Northern English words like *bairn* (child), *bide* (stay), *wee* (small)
- *blether* (chatter), *kirk* (church), *lug* (ear), *lass* (girl) are originally Scandinavian
- French borrowings include *tassie* (cup, Fr. tasse), *ashet* (serving dish, Fr. assiette), *Hogmanay* (New Year celebration, Fr. aguilleneuf – a New year's gift), *vennel* (alley, Fr. venelle)
- other borrowings include *bog, glen, loch, slogan* (war-cry), *brogue* from Gaelic, *pinkie* (little finger), *close* (entry passage in a tenement), *advocate* (barrister).

Welsh English

Although English is the majority language in Wales today, the Welsh have reason to be hostile towards it, since English was the invading language in Wales at the time of the Norman Conquest, displacing the native Celtic language. Welsh has a long and distinguished literary tradition, but this was not enough to protect the language in the twentieth century from the further encroaching of English via the media and population shifts. The Welsh Language Act (1967) signalled a halt in the rapid decline in Welsh, and there has been a gradual turnaround since. Welsh is now the medium of instruction in some schools, and taught in all schools. It continues to be spoken mainly in the north west; in Wales as a whole there are approximately 25% bilingual Welsh–English speakers.

The extent to which *Welsh English* is influenced by the Welsh language depends on where people live – close to the border with England, in the south east or in the more isolated Welsh-speaking north west.

Pronunciation

- vowels are less differentiated than in RP; intonation patterns are more sing-song and varied because of the rise-fall intonation at the end of an utterance; syllable stress is more even, instead of the variable stress of RP; /h/ is often missed at the beginning of a word
- consonants that are typical of Welsh English are the voiceless ɬ sound of /ɬ/ *Llangollen, Llandudno*, the voiceless r sound as in *Rhyl* and the ʝ /x/ sound, as in *bach, Pentyrch,*

Grammar

- word order change as in *Running late I am for the class, Exhausted I am*; additional tag *isn't it* as in *You've finished that book, isn't it?* (NB *look you* is a tag not as frequently used as people think); the use of *there* as in *There's late you are after all that*; plus the non-standard grammatical usage found in English (multiple negation etc).

Vocabulary

- terms of address include *bach* (dear), *boyo*; Welsh words *eisteddfod* (cultural festival), *iechyd da* (good health), *nain, taid* (grandma, grandpa).

Irish English

Crystal points out that Ireland was the first of the *overseas* English-speaking colonies where English has been spoken for over 800 years. *Gaelic* (the Irish rather than the Scottish version) was the language of Ireland at the moment of invasion in the twelfth century; it is still spoken in the West of Ireland (the Gaeltacht), is an official language of the Irish Republic, and is studied in school to the age of 16. Even so, English is the dominant language in both Northern Ireland and Eire, and *Irish English* has spread worldwide because of the migrations.

Irish English includes *Anglo-Irish*, which is the educated middle-class usage; *Ulster Scots* or *Ullans*, which is the Scottish-influenced usage of Antrim, Donegal and Down with over 150,000 speakers in the nine counties; and *Hiberno-English*, which is a Gaelic-influenced predominantly working-class usage.

Pronunciation

- vowels like /ei:/ as in *tea* are pronounced *tay*; *join* is pronounced as *jine*; stress patterns are often different from RP (stress comes later in the word as in *orchestra, diagnose, Belfast*)
- consonants: (*th*) as in *thin* is pronounced as /t/ *tín*; (*th*) as in *this* can be pronounced as /d/ *dis*; before consonants like /t/, /n/ and /l/ the sibilant /s/ can become (*sh*) so *stop* becomes *shtop*.

Grammar

- *youse* for plural pronoun *you*; *but* used instead of *though* at the end of a sentence *I don't want it but*; emphatic *it is so* in response to a question; questions are repeated *will you have this? I will not have it*; imperative *let you be staying here now*; questions used as answers *Can you tell the way to the station? – Will it be the parcel office or the trains you'll be wanting?* There are many more of these expressions (see Crystal, p.338).

Vocabulary

- *bold* (naughty); *garda* (police); *greet* (weep: Scots); *spalpeen* (rascal) and many others.

ACTIVITY 29

Most of us know someone who is Scottish, Welsh or Irish in origin. If possible, choose someone you know reasonably well who is willing to be recorded in an informal interview about a topic like childhood, school, holidays etc. Record the interview (about 15–20 minutes in length), having taken a brief linguistic history from your interviewee (ie place of birth, place of parents' birth, length of time lived in one area, other languages spoken). Listen to the tape carefully two or three times; then note down any examples of typical *pronunciation, grammar* or *vocabulary* (described above), or any other spoken language features you have observed.

American English

The English who colonised the Eastern seaboard in the late sixteenth and early seventeenth centuries spoke mainly North and East Midlands pronunciation and dialect forms, but wrote established standard form.

The steady expansion westwards over 100 years means that there are few real differences between American regional accents, apart from the marked difference between Southern and 'General American' accents. Southern accents, interestingly, have produced the same kind of *negative attitudes* as we have noticed in relation to Northern accents in England (Northern accents are associated with the industrial working class, Southern accents with hillbillies and hicks). The long drawling Southern vowels (e.g. *ahss tay*

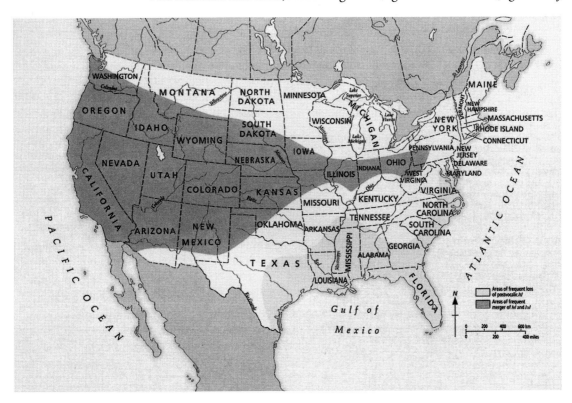

'ice tea'; *haagwaash* 'hog-wash'; *yall* 'you all') make Southern speech hard for non-Southerners to understand. Some Southerners find their accent awkward too; a visiting linguist noticed evening classes on 'How to Control Your Southern Accent' . . .

As we see above, there are three broad dialect areas in the USA (Northern, Southern, Midland), and some significant regional variations in urban as well as rural locations. Across America there is also the *Black American English dialect*, sometimes called *Afro-American English*, sometimes *Black English Vernacular* or *BEV* (Labov), and lately called *Ebonics* (*ebony* + phon*ics*). In 1997 in California there was a movement to have this recognised as a separate language from American Standard English, but it was a short-lived proposal, overcome by standardising and normative pressures (see p.34–35).

There are many dialect differences in vocabulary across America. For example, a long bread roll filled with meat, cheese etc. has many different regional names: *poorboy* (New Orleans); *hoagy* (Philadelphia); *hero* (New York City); *submarine* (Boston); *grinder* (upstate New York) – and there will be others elsewhere.

Pronunciation: General American

- the long /a:/ of RP in *bath, advance, sample, laugh, past* is shortened to /a/
- /r/ is pronounced at the end of a word everywhere except New York City, eastern New England and the Southern states
- /j/ (in RP pronunciation) is lost in words like *duke* /du:k/, and *tune* /tu:n/ but kept in words like *value, menu*
- the vowels in *caught* and *cot* are close together in pronunciation; /d/ tends to replace (*tt*) or (*t*) as in *letter* /leder/, *metal* /medl/, *latter* /lader/
- there are many differences from RP in the stressing of syllables (eg **add**ress, **lab**oratory, adver**tise**ment, **contro**versy, **inqui**ry).

Spelling differences include: -ize instead of -ise (*realize/realise, analyze/analyse*); -er instead of -re (*center/centre*); -or instead of -our (*honor/honour, color/colour*); -og instead of -ogue (*catalog/catalogue*), together with other individual differences (eg *check/cheque; defense/defence; woolen/woollen; donut/doughnut; drafty/draughty; jewelry/jewellery*.

Grammar

- Americans prefer *have* to British 'have got' (*do you have the time? I don't*)
- word order difference: *Hudson River*/River Thames; *a half hour*/half an hour
- different preposition usage: *half after four*/half past four; *it's a quarter of three*/a quarter to three; *they live on 43rd and Fifth*/they live in Green Street
- the verb *gotten* has several meanings: 'obtained' (*I've gotten a new coat*); 'managed to achieve something' (*I've gotten to enjoy cycling in London in spite of the fumes*); 'become' (*I've gotten interested in chess*); 'moved' (*she's gotten off that topic at last*)
- in some dialects double modals are used (*might it could happen; might have could have been there; used to wouldn't do it*)

- local American dialect can be similar to English dialect usage (*a-peddling, a-have, a-doing, wait on, right good*)
- some irregular past tense forms (*dove/dived; snuck/sneaked; fit/fitted*)
- new verbs created by adding the suffix *-ize, -ify* (*burglarize, hospitalize, beautify*)
- word class switching (especially noun to verb) to *author* a book, to *action* a plan, to *host* a meeting.

Vocabulary

- American neologisms created (*to go on the warpath, to bury the hatchet*)
- borrowings from *Amerindian* languages (*raccoon, moccasin, skunk, wigwam, canoe, squaw*) as well as place-names (*Delaware, Susquehanna, Manhattan, Idaho, Mississippi*)
- borrowings from *other colonial languages*: French (*prairie, bureau, bayou* and place-names *St Louis, Baton Rouge, New Orleans*); Dutch (*waffle, cookie, boss* and place-names *Schuylkill, Schenectady, Conshohocken*); Spanish (*lasso, ranch* and place-names *Florida, Los Angeles, San Francisco, Santa Barbara*)
- borrowings from *immigrant languages*: Japanese (*sukiyaki*); German (*noodle, dumb, hamburger*); Swedish (*smorgasbord*)
- English words with new meanings (*creek* means small stream, not small coastal estuary).

ACTIVITY 30

1 Films or television tend to provide the best opportunities for hearing different American accents. Examples of films include: *Fargo* (North Dakota), *Cat on a Hot Tin Roof* and *Gone with the Wind* (South); *Paris, Texas* (South West); *The Graduate* (California); *Manhattan Murder Mystery* and *Bullets over Broadway* (New York). Television chat shows (*Oprah Winfrey, Springer*) provide opportunities to hear *ordinary* people talking.

Choose a film or television show and record a short extract. Listen to your recording and find examples of characteristic American pronunciation. Then working with a partner try to *accurately* reproduce an American accent, and record your conversation.

2 Many English people argue that Americanisms are too dominant in English today. Select *one* article *each* from a tabloid newspaper, a broadsheet newspaper and a fashion or music-based magazine, and list the American usages in each article.

Caribbean English (West Indian English, Black British English)

The word *Caribbean* reminds us of the history of the Carib people who first inhabited the West Indies, sharing them with the Arawak people. Their languages are still spoken in the islands, but much more dominant are the languages of the European colonists (English, French and Spanish). *English* is spoken in Jamaica, Barbados, the Virgin Islands; *French* in Haiti and Martinique, *Spanish* and *Portuguese* in Puerto Rico, Cuba, the Dominican Republic; *Dutch* in the Antilles. (Look at the place-names to discover the colonial past of each island.) The West African languages *Ewe* and *Yoruba* were introduced to the Caribbean by the slaves shipped over to work in the plantations.

The languages that evolved on each island as a result of contact between the colonial language and the African languages are called **creoles**. When people speaking two different languages have to communicate, two things happen. First a basic language (**pidgin**) develops, with simple grammar and limited vocabulary. Second, a generation later, this simplified language gains the normal complexity of every human language, and then becomes a **creole** language. We shall be looking at some English creoles (Caribbean and elsewhere) later in this chapter.

Is there such a thing as Standard West Indian English? It's possible that although local variations of Caribbean English are spoken in Jamaica, Barbados, the Virgin Islands, Trinidad and Guyana, a standard form is emerging (Crystal, 1995 p.344). On each island there is a *creole continuum* with *West Indian Standard English* at one end and an *English creole language* at the other. People switch along the continuum depending on social context and level of formality.

Pronunciation

- evenly stressed syllables (eg *Jam ai ca* ; *dis app oint* ; *in ter fere*)
- *cat, cot, caught* all sound the same (vowels /a/ and /o/ merge)
- *fear* and *fare* sound the same (dipthongs /iə/ and /ɛə/ merge)
- RP /ei/ as in *cake* in Jamaica but /e:/ as in 'keek' on other English-speaking islands
- RP /əu/ as in *coat* is /uɒ/ in Jamaica but /o:/ on other islands
- /t/ replaces /th/ (*thin* becomes *tin*), /d/ replaces /th/ (*this* becomes *dis*); /r/ is rhotic (pronounced) in words like *car, hard*
- final consonant clusters often simplified *bes'* for *best*, *wok'* for *walked*
- consonants assimilated or elided (/a: redi/ for *already*)
- consonants can be reversed *sandals* becomes /slandaz/; *ask* becomes /aks/.

Grammar

- *would* is preferred to *will* (*I would do that tomorrow*)
- *get* is used as a passive (*that vase get break*)
- questions indicated by intonation only (*You finish that now?*).

Vocabulary

Loan words come from: French (*fete* – picnic; *macommere* – godmother or close female friend); Spanish (*armadillo*); Arawak (*iguana*); Carib (*manatee* – sea cow); West African languages (*bakra, buckra* – a white person). Other familiar words include *calypso, ganja* (cannabis) and *rasta* (Rastafarian). There are also a large number of local variants, most of which are not known to people on other English-speaking islands.

ACTIVITY 31

Listen to recordings of a poet like Grace Nichols (Guyanese) or Derek Walcott (St. Lucian) to learn to recognise differences between different Caribbean Englishes – or ask a friend to help you.

Australian English

We're familiar with *Australian English* because of films like *Crocodile Dundee*, comedians like Barry Humphries (creator of Dame Edna Everage, Sir Les Patterson and Barry Mackenzie) and Australian television 'soaps' like *Neighbours* and *Home and Away*. There's even a comic version of Australian, *Strine* (say it aloud and you'll get the meaning).

Australia was originally a penal colony (though there were always some free settlers), first established in 1788. The new arrivals, virtually all English speaking, encountered the indigenous Aboriginal peoples, all speaking a huge variety of languages. We already know some of the linguistic consequences and there are many others, political, social and economic.

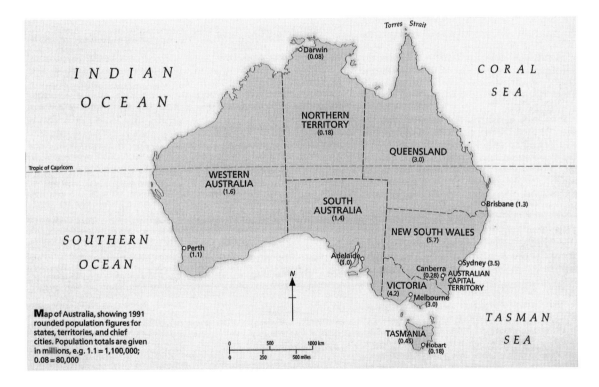

Map of Australia, showing 1991 rounded population figures for states, territories, and chief cities. Population totals are given in millions, e.g. 1.1 = 1,100,000; 0.08 = 80,000

Pronunciation

There are three different Australian accents: *Cultivated, Broad* and *General,* which derive from the regional accents of the early settlers. The *Cultivated accent* (used by 10% of the population) is close to RP and is associated with education and the literary establishment (as used by Germaine Greer); *Broad Australian* (used by 30%) is the accent of 'Dame Edna' and 'Sir Les Patterson'; *General* is the familiar mainstream accent (used by 60%) we hear on television soaps.

- /eɪ/ becomes /aɪ/ as in 'Austrilia' (*Australia*) or 'gedai' (*g'day*)
- *now* /naʊ/ sounds more open, with the short /a/ emphasised
- in words like *now* and *down* the vowels are strongly nasalised, producing

a typical Australian 'twang' (Crystal); the consonant /r/ is not pronounced

- *high rising tone* or *AQI* (*Australian Questioning Intonation*) at the end of a clause. According to Guy and Vonwiller (1986) this is a recent intonation change used especially by young working-class women, and continuing to spread. It's been suggested that this use of a questioning tone in a statement is either a way of testing the *listener's understanding* of what's been said (*You know how much I dislike mashed potato*), or it might be an expression of female linguistic insecurity (see Chapters 3 & 4).

Grammar

- no significant regional variation; some immigrant grammatical forms (*youse* – Irish).

Vocabulary

- English words applied to different situations (*bush* for native vegetation)
- Aboriginal words (*kookaburra* – a native bird; *kangeroo, boomerang, billabong, dingo, koala* and place-names *Woollongong, Wagga Wagga, Kalgoorlie*)
- new words (*outback, walkabout, gold-rush, prospector, claim, station* or *ranch*)
- slang terms: *tinnie* (tin of beer), *arvo* (afternoon), *sheila* (girl), *pommy* (British person), *cobber* (friend) *crook* (ill), *to shoot through* (leave), *dag* (amusing person), *to shout* (pay for a friend), *drongo* (fool)
- general terms: *pavlova, flying doctor, barbie, weekender* (holiday cottage).

ACTIVITY 32

Record any episode from an Australian soap opera. Select a 10-minute extract and note the use of *Australian Questioning Intonation* by the characters. Is there any difference in usage in relation to age group or gender? Compare your findings with other members of the group.

Indian English

English is one of 15 major languages spoken in India (others include Hindi, Bengali, Tamil, Gujerati, Urdu, Kannada, Marathi and Punjabi). The term *Indian English* implies one variety, but it covers *Boxwallah* or *'kitchen'* English, *Anglo-Indian English* as well as *British English*.

English has been used in India for nearly 400 years. Shortly after the East India Company was established in 1600, English traders settled in major cities like Surat, Bombay, Madras and Calcutta. By the eighteenth century British missionaries were establishing English-speaking schools, and when direct British rule replaced the East India Company in 1859, English became even more important as the language of the British Raj. It had already been decided that English should be the medium of education at university level, and three English-medium universities were established at Bombay, Calcutta and Madras.

English was the language of the elite, and remained so, even after independence (1947). Today, according to MacArthur, English is spoken regularly by over 30 million Indian people with differing degrees of competence.

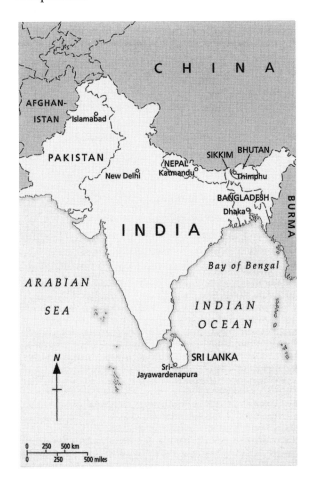

Hindi is the official language of India, and English is the associate official language. Although it is used in the legal system, in administration, in the military, business, the media and education, for no Indian speaker is English their mother-tongue. This can result in *language interference* (p.44).

Pronunciation

- syllable-timed (all syllables given equal weight *hosp it al it y*)
- /th/ (*three*) pronounced as *t* (*t'ree*); /th/ (*those*) becomes *d* (*doze*); /f/ (*food*) becomes *p* (*pood*)
- no distinction between /w/ (*wish*) and /v/ (*vine* is pronounced as wine)
- /r/ is pronounced.

Grammar

- stative verbs (to be, to seem, to become) used in the progressive or continuous form (*I am answering you, she is understanding your problem*)

- tag response *isn't it* (*shall we go now, isn't it?*); *itself* or *only* used to replace question intonation (*you must be in this place tomorrow itself; he arrived today only*)
- inconsistent use of determiners (*train has gone; inconvenience is great; the worrying does no good*) probably the result of *language interference*, where the determiner and noun are one word, as in Punjabi
- present perfect used instead of simple past (*I have written that letter yesterday*)
- pluralising of English mass nouns (*we ate fruits all day; there is too much litters*)
- different preposition in phrasal verbs (*to dispense* meaning 'do without'; *to return back; to pay attention on*)
- unusual noun compounding (*key-bunch; bottle-water; pindrop silence*)
- *interference* from Indian languages affecting grammar (eg omission of determiner described above).

Vocabulary

- words from Indian languages include *bungalow, calico, cheetah, chit, chutney, jodphurs, juggernaut, pukka, pundit, sahib, rupee, mogul, guru, nirvana, yoga, verandah, jungle, coolie, juice*
- English/Indian compound nouns (*brahminhood, tiffin* [lunch] *box*)
- idiomatic expressions eg *to sit on someone's neck* meaning 'to watch them carefully'.

ACTIVITY 33

1 We encounter *Indian English* in the British Asian community and in film and television representations (*Bhaji on the Beach, Goodness Gracious Me!, Mississippi Masala*).

Write a review of a film or television programme you have seen in which some variety of Indian English is used, focusing particularly on the use of dialogue.

2 Look up the following Englishes in Crystal or McArthur (see Further Reading): *South African English, Canadian English, New Zealand English, Singaporean English*. Make notes on pronunciation, grammar, vocabulary on the model used here to complete your study of *Different Englishes*.

English creoles

There are three major groups of *English creoles*: **Atlantic creoles** (Caribbean, North America); **West African creoles** (West African coast); **South East Asian creoles** (China coast, New Guinea, Australia). These creoles resulted from trading or slavery contact between English and local languages.

A more detailed look at the process of creolisation

As we have seen (p.54), *creolisation* means the single generation process from the simplified language system of a *pidgin* to a *creole*. This process can be fast or slow, depending on whether the language goes straight to *creole*, or moves through the stages of *stabilised* and *expanded pidgin* first. In *creolisation* there is always a dominant language called the **superstrate** or **lexifier language** and a weaker one called the **substrate language**. In English creoles English is the superstrate or lexifier language. **Decreolisation** can also take place, when a creole moves back towards the *lexifier language* (ie the one from which most of its *lexis* is drawn). An example of this process is *Black American English*, which was once a creole, but is now thought of as a variety of American English.

Do all creoles have features in common?

Bickerton (1981) would say yes. He argues that *all* creoles have common features because they represent an early stage in the universal process of **language acquisition**. Some linguists think that creoles developed from an early trading language called *Sabir*. Others argue that whatever the lexifier language, it sets the **standard form** or **acrolect**. English creoles do have some features in common (see below):

- use negative *before* verb in SVO structure (*he no want bread*)
- make no distinction between *active* and *passive* voice (*dem **plaan** di tri* 'they planted the tree'; *di tri **plaan*** 'the tree was planted' [MacArthur])
- use intonation only to ask questions (no word order change)
- verb *to be* often omitted and adjectives used as verbs or adverbs (*she real sick*).

Atlantic Creoles (Jamaican and American)

The Caribbean creoles include **Jamaican**, **Barbadian**, **Bahamian**, **Trinebagian** and **Guyanese creoles**; further north a creole called **Gullah** is spoken along the eastern coast of Florida, Georgia and the Carolinas.

Jamaican creole is one of the most familiar creoles because it is spoken in the UK, as well as in Jamaica. It is sometimes called **patois**; in the UK it is spoken bilingually with English, usually in informal contexts (Crystal, 1995 p.347). Recently, it has gained popularity among white teenagers ('wiggers') who enjoy using it with their West Indian friends. Characteristics include:

- no agreement between subject and verb (*she walk in de rain*)
- verb placed at front of sentence for emphasis (*a grumble John grumble make he trouble*)
- several verbs used closely together (*she talk say you clever*)
- particles *da, di, a* used to show continuous action (*he da work now*)
- past tense uses base form (*he run*); *done* expresses completed action (*he just done run*); *been* can also express past action (*they been gone*)

- nouns tend not to use the plural marker -s (*three chicken, dem bird*); the particle *dem* indicates plurality
- the particle *fi* expresses possession (*dat book a fi me*); or sometimes nouns are placed next to each other (*dat man dog*) also to express possession
- no change in pronouns in subject, object or possessive positions (*she give they she answer*)
- alternative pronouns *mi/ I* (I), *a/ im/ he* (he), *i/ yu/ yunu* (you plural), *del dem* (they)
- auxiliary *do* not used with question (*why you say no*).

West African Creoles

These include **Sierra Leone Krio**, **Gambian Creole**, **Ghanaian Pidgin English** and are similar to Atlantic creoles in pronunciation and grammar. Because English is the official language of Ghana, Sierra Leone, Nigeria, Gambia and Cameroon, it is used as a second, third or fourth language and has gained many loan words from *Yoruba, Hausa* and *Twi*. *West African Creole English* is the **acrolect** (prestige form); *West African Pidgin English* is the **mesolect** (form used by most people) and the **basilect** is close to the original African language.

South East Asian Creoles

English-based creoles in South East Asia are predominantly coastal or island languages, the best known being **Tok Pisin** (Papua New Guinea) and **Bislama** (Vanuatu/New Hebrides).

Tok Pisin (Talk Pidgin)

Tok Pisin is the **lingua franca** in Papua New Guinea (this means a language everyone can speak and understand). This creole evolved through contact between English-speaking Europeans (including Australians) and Pacific Islanders in the late nineteenth century.

Grammar

- *two* first person plural pronouns: *yumi* (meaning both the speaker and the addressee) and *mipela* (speaker and any others *not* addressed)
- *-pela* (fellow) is added to adjectives (eg *gutpela man* – good man; *naispela haus* – nice house; *wanpela* – 'one')
- *-im* is used as a verb ending (*askim* – to question; *lukautim* – to take care of; *bagarapim* – to ruin, damage, 'bugger up'; *tokim* – to tell)
- *bilong* is used to show possession (*bilong mi* – mine)
- pronouns *mi* – I, me; *em* – he, him; *yupela* – you.

Vocabulary

- *pikinini* (child, cf. Jamaican Creole *picanninny*); *meri* (woman); *olgeta* (altogether); *long* (along); *na* (and); *nau* (now); *tasol* (but, that's all).

Bislama

In 1980 the islands of the New Hebrides (discovered by Captain James Cook in 1774) were renamed the republic of Vanuatu. Bislama, English and French are Vanuatu's three official languages, with Bislama the *lingua franca*. The name *Bislama* (*beche la mer*) means 'beach of the sea', and it is similar to *Tok Pisin* in vocabulary and grammar.

Grammar

- *-fala* is the adjective suffix (*wanfala man* means 'a man')
- *-em* used as a transitive verb marker
- *-I* or *-oli* mark the verb phrase or predicate of each clause (*hem oli faenem pikinini* – she found the child)
- as in *Tok Pisin*, words can be reduplicated (*toktok* – talk; *lukluk* – look)
- future tense marker is *bambae*
- as in *Tok Pisin*, *save* (know) is used as a modal verb like *may, might, can.*

ACTIVITY 34

Below are four extracts from Jamaican Creole, Guyanese Creole, Tok Pisin and Bislama. Rewrite each extract in Standard English (you may need to say aloud words you find hard to understand). Then compare the use of
a) personal pronouns and b) verb forms. Are there any similarities between an Atlantic Creole and a South Asian Creole?

1 Jamaican Creole

The following extract is a conversation between two teenage girls **J** and **C**. Both were born in London and have Jamaican parents (the numbers in brackets represent the length of pause in minutes and seconds).

C: She invite you?

J: No

C: She never invite me neither and Leonie 'ave one as well never invite never tell me noin' (0.4) me no business too

J: Leonie have party?

C: Man (1.0) Leonie have party (0.4) when? (1.2) don' remember when it was but she did tell all o' dem no fi- t say not'in' (0.6) cau' she no wan' too much Cyatford gyal de dere (1.0) an' Jackie 'ave one too (0.4) never say not'in'
(Source: Mark Sebba (1993) *London Jamaican* Longman p.20)

2 Guyanese Creole

The speaker is an 80-year-old woman reminiscing about her childhood.

A riimembo wen o woz o chaild, a krismostaim, di fos faiyo ai sii in gayana. Ai in noo wo yeer wuz do. A heer waan skwib, an from do di priven skwib from komin in di konchrii. Waan skwib – di chainii di duuwin skwib tu – tu Leopool schriit kaarno an Lambord schriit. An di hool plees bloo op!
(Source: Rickford (1987) p. 250, cited in *Open University Study Guide 1, The English Language: past, present and future*)

3 Tok Pisin

The speakers are **M** (manager) and **D** (member of staff).

M: Yu kolim nem bilong yu?

D: Nem bilong mi, D . . .

M: Yu marit?

D: Nogat, mi no marit, mi stap nating

M: Tasol yu slip wi?

D: Mi slip wantaim brata bilong mi long Boroko

M: Bilong wanem?

D: Bilong mi no gat haus bilong mi yet

M: Yu gat haumas krismas?

D: Mi no save. Ating mi gat samting olsem tupela ten sikis

M: Orait, nau yu ken I go na kirapim wok
(Source: T. E. Dutton (1973) *Conversational New Guinea Pidgin*, Pacific Linguistics Series D No 12, The Australian National University p.107)

4 Bislama

This is taken from a broadcast interview. **G** and **M** are discussing government loans for farmers.

G: Gud ivning evriwan. M … mi harem plante pipol oli tokbaut samting oli kolem agrikaljaral lon. Wanem nao samting ya?

M: Long Niu Hebridis hem I gat mane we I save givim long ol pipol we I wantem mekem gud wok long agrikalja. Oli kolem lon, from we taem ol pipol oli tekem aot mane oli mas pem bak afta long Kondominiom.

G: Sipos mi askem sam mane from lon ya, wanem nao mi save yusum long mane we mi askem?

M: Yu save yusum mane ya long eni wok long agrikalja or faming blong yu we yu wantem mekem gud. Wan gud samting, yu save pem waea taem makim fenis raon long kokonas plantesin blong yu …

(Source: YELSA (York English Language Studies Associates) Series 3 Topic 2 Unit 6)

Learning English

Speakers of other languages have a variety of reasons for wanting to learn English. They may live in a society where government policy requires fluency in English, or where English is a *lingua franca*, or they want to access the Internet. Whatever the reason, teaching English to non-native speakers is a huge industry worldwide. Here is a selection of some of the acronyms for English language teaching today:

- EFL (English as a Foreign Language)
- TEFL (Teaching English as a Foreign Language)
- EAP (English for Academic Purposes)
- EIL (English as an International Language)
- ESL (English as a Second Language)
- ESP (English for Special Purposes)
- ESOL (English for Speakers of Other Languages)
- TESOL (Teaching English to Speakers of Other Languages)

These programmes are primarily targeted at different adult client groups, such as business people, potential students at British or American universities, or new arrivals in the UK or America. Courses are offered at beginner, intermediate and advanced levels and students gain recognised qualifications. In some countries English is the *teaching medium* (e.g. India, Malaysia, Hong Kong); in others it is taught as a *foreign language*.

Teaching strategies range from formal translation and grammar study, to more informal conversation-based methods. All aim to provide the learner with *communicative competence* in English. More recently there has been emphasis on the understanding of *language functions* as well as *language forms*, and on recognising the importance of context, levels of formality and appropriacy of content.

Many countries have language policies today to ensure that indigenous languages are supported and not destroyed as a result of increasing demand for English, and to avoid the possibility of **linguistic imperialism** happening all over again!

ACTIVITY 35

Imagine you have been asked to write part of an Open Learning unit intended to teach beginners about a point of English grammar. Choose your grammar point (forming plurals, forming the passive, word order etc) and write out your section of the unit, making it as interesting and accessible as possible.

Summary

We have looked at the global role of English today, at different Englishes and English creoles, at the problems and responsibilities associated with the teaching and learning of English, and at the range of attitudes held towards English at the beginning of the new millennium. Ultimately, English is nothing more than just another vehicle for human communication – its huge influence today derives from its past. Will it be able to sustain an international role in an increasingly multilingual community without destroying the magnificent range of human languages still existing today?

Further reading

Goodman, S. and Graddol, D. (1996) *Redesigning English: new texts, new identities* Open University Press and Routledge

Graddol, D. Leith D. and Swann J. (1996) *English: history, diversity and change* Open University Press and Routledge

Labov, William (1972) *Language in the Inner City* University of Pennsylvania Press

McArthur, Tom (1996) *The Oxford Companion to the English Language* Oxford University Press

McArthur, Tom (1998) *The English Languages* Cambridge University Press

Sebba, Mark (1993) *London Jamaican* Longman

Trudgill, P. and Hannah, J. (1985) *International English* Arnold

3 Representations of Difference: Identity

We all have a sense of individuality, of identity, of difference, of uniqueness, expressed in the way we speak and write. The first two chapters have focused on the effects of society and its linguistic practices on people, and on the way that social, regional and economic factors affect our *own* use of language and our attitudes to *other people's* use of language.

We shall now take a different angle, and swing the spotlight round to focus, not on society, but on the *individuals* who make up society, not at people in general but at the individual *self* in particular. We shall try to discover to what extent our individual *identity* and *idiolect* are affected by two basic factors: *age* and *gender*. Other factors (*family structure, education* and *ethnicity*) are important, but less central to our purpose here. We shall investigate not only the ways in which age and gender affect our spoken and written language as *private individuals*, but also how they are **represented** in the *public domain*. You may recall the powerful influence of *attitudes* and *stereotypes* on language use discussed in Chapter 1. Will similar patterns emerge in this context?

The Self

When does our sense of self emerge?

One of the most dramatic changes in a baby's development is at the age of approximately 12–13 months. Suddenly the child becomes aware of being an individual who is *separate*, not attached to a mother, father or caregiver. This is terrifying! The friendly, jolly baby who 'would go to anyone' hides away from strangers, refuses to leave the security of a friendly lap, and cries when a parent leaves the room. But this is a *crucial* moment in the child's psychological and linguistic development, in that it marks the dawning of a sense of *self*. As we mature, our sense of self, of individual identity, continues to develop (hopefully not too much battered by life experience) and during adolescence gradually becomes solid and established. We begin to understand what makes us uniquely human.

ACTIVITY 36

1 Write down *six* things about yourself which sum you up as a unique individual (they could be to do with your appearance, your family background, your temperament, the way you behave, your age or gender, your likes and dislikes etc).

2 Compare notes with a friend – if you don't want to reveal anything, just identify the *categories* selected. Whatever you have written indicates a sense of your self as a unique person. You may well have selected age and gender as significant categories.

How is our sense of self established?

A sense of individual self develops in a variety of ways. We are presented with images of ourselves by people who know us well, and in the outside world we may be influenced by media *representations* of people like ourselves. The way people *act towards us* is another mirror of the self; and so is the way people *react* to us. The long journey to self-discovery is a constant process of mirroring other people's attitudes (and exploring our own) to this mysterious concept of 'self', the ultimate means of differentiation. It is obvious that *age* and *gender* will always be important factors in this process, since they are the two 'givens' that exist at the beginning of life, and last till the moment of death.

Throughout our life, our identity is expressed in a multitude of ways – but one of the most significant is the way we use language.

Age as a sociolinguistic variable

There is a tendency when we use the word 'age' to associate it with the last stages of human life, which in Western industrial society usually means post-retirement. But logically speaking, the term can apply to any stage in life, from infancy to adulthood and beyond. Nor is chronological age necessarily in step with social and biological development, although we expect it to be. Indeed, if people's behaviour differs from expected age norms, there are disparaging comments ('don't be such a baby', 'she's behaving like a teenager', 'he's middle-aged already at sixteen!', 'you're such an old woman!'). An interesting question – does each person's *idiolect* change in the course of a lifetime, as their *speech community* changes, or does linguistic individuality remain the same throughout life?

Popular attitudes to age

Age group is a term used to refer to everyone at a similar chronological stage in life, from babies learning the rudiments of speech to elderly people who may have problems of language dysfunction. Each age group has its own (often stereotyped) language characteristics. For example, in Britain at the start of the new millennium, elderly people will not only remember the Second World War, but also the wartime slang of their youth. And the 1960s teenage generation – now thoroughly middle-aged – may even retain the vocabulary of the so-called 'permissive society' (*flower power, drug culture, the permissive society, the Swinging Sixties*). Similarly the language of today's generation of teenagers is likely to be highly computer oriented, whether it's Pokemon, computer games or e-mail text messaging.

People can be surprisingly intolerant of the characteristic language of other age groups. At home, where different age groups have to communicate, the older generation tends to demand conformity to *their* language usage ('don't use bad language to me!', 'talk properly!', 'I don't know *what* you're talking about', 'why don't you speak up?'). In the world outside, our old friend the *complaint tradition* (see p.35) appears (e.g. 'why do people use all these American spellings?', 'News-readers today aren't what they used to be – did you hear his accent?').

To sum up: **age** and **generation** *do* make a difference to our individual *idiolect*, **and** to our sense of *self* and *identity*, **and** to our *attitudes* to other people's language.

ACTIVITY 37

Identify *two* people of different generations whom you know well (perhaps someone from your parents' generation, and someone from your grandparents' generation). Write down in advance a few questions to find out:

1   what popular slang they used when they were younger, and whether they still use it (ask

about schooldays, friendships, relationships, public events etc). Keep careful notes of all the terms mentioned.

2   what annoys them about the language of younger generations (collect as many examples as possible).

Linguistics and age

The linguist **Penelope Eckert** points out that each of us has our own *linguistic life course*, and that at each stage (infancy, early childhood, adolescence, young adulthood, middle age, old age) *language use* can be studied. Most 'age' research has been focused on child language development, with a few important studies on adolescent language (Labov, 1972; Cheshire, 1982; Eckert, 1997), but very little has been done on adult language, and even less on old people's language. However, things began to change with the landmark publication of **Coupland and Giles** (1991) *Language, Society and the Elderly*. Our focus here will be on two linguistic life stages: *adolescence* and *old age*.

Language and adolescence/young adulthood

Adolescence is a Western concept which has emerged because we keep our young people artificially removed from adult society in secondary and tertiary education. Western young people tend to be economically inactive (apart from part-time jobs), and are usually not expected to undertake adult roles in society until their education is complete.

The *language of adolescents* often reflects their need to define themselves as separate from the adult world, and to create their own social group by preferring non-standard language, especially slang, taboo and anti-language. Labov was one of the first linguists to investigate the language of adolescents (black New York gang members – the Jets, Cobras and the Thunderbirds); more recent studies include Jenny Cheshire's work on Reading teenagers' language (see Chapter 1, p.22).

Labov aimed to find out why young Black Americans had significant reading problems, but his findings revealed more about Black American Vernacular as a richly effective language (ranging from the way gang structure affected language, to the use of ritual insults, called 'sounding'). He concluded that the young Black Americans' reading problems were linked with their social and political deprivation, and that their language was just as effective in *communicative competence* as any other adolescent language.

The following extract comes from Labov's data and is an account of a fight (*Language in the Inner City*, University of Pennsylvania Press, 1972, pp.358–9):

Interviewer: What was the most important fight you remember?

John L: Well, one (I think) was with a girl.
Like I was a kid, you know,
And she was the baddest girl, *the baddest girl in the neighbourhood*
If you didn't bring her candy to school, she would punch you in the mouth:

And you had to kiss her when she'd tell you

This girl was only about 12 years old, man, but she was a killer.
She didn't take no junk;
She whupped all her brothers.
And I came to school one day
And I didn't have no money.
My ma wouldn't give me no money.
And I played hookies one day,
[She] put something on me (*hit me hard*).
I played hookies, man,
so I said, you know, I'm not going to play hookies no more
'cause I don't wanna get a whupping.
So I go to school
and this girl says 'Where's the candy?'
I said, 'I don't have it.'
She says, powww!
So I says to myself, 'There's gonna be times my mother won't give me money

because [we're] a poor family

And I can't take this all, you know, every time she don't give me any money.'
So I say, 'Well, I just gotta fight this girl.
She gonna hafta whup me.

I hope she don't whup me.'
And I hit the girl: powwww!
And I put something on it.
I win the fight.
That was one of the most important.

ACTIVITY 38

1 Analyse the narrative above, identifying examples of non-standard lexical and grammatical usage. How effective is it as a narrative?

2 Record a group of young people talking informally for long enough to avoid the *Observer's Paradox* effect (see p.6). Plan carefully before recording – will you get a varied range of conversation? Does your data confirm the descriptions of young people's language given above?

3 Record an informal interview with a young person on a topic you think will encourage him or her to talk freely. You could try Labov's strategy (*Were you ever in a situation where you thought you were in serious danger?*) or ask your subject to talk about the most frightening/exciting/happy occasion that he or she remembers. Listen carefully to your recording and write a short report on their lexical choice, *comparing* it with the lexical choice of your subjects in Q2 above.

NB Adolescent fiction might be an interesting area for a *language investigation*. Writers who are trying to create a realistic impression of young people's speech usually use a mixture of standard, non-standard lexis and slang. Look at literary portraits of young adults like Holden Caulfield (*The Catcher in the Rye*), Adrian Mole (*The Diary of Adrian Mole Aged 13¾*) or the invented language of the psychopathic hero in *Brighton Rock*.

Language and old age

How do we define *old age*? When does it begin? To say that it means the period between stopping work and dying sounds blunt, but is relatively accurate. People normally retire between the ages of 60 (women) and 65 (men). Many people have more than 20 years of active life left, depending on health, social and economic circumstances. Linguists who study the language of old people group their subjects either in decades, or in 'life experience' groups (people who shared wartime experience, either as adults or children). This enables them to study the linguistic effects of change over time on selected individuals, or on people living in the same social unit (eg nursing home, retirement community, geriatric hospital).

Coupland *et al* (1991) use the conventional but helpful distinction between 'young-old' people (up to mid 70s) and 'old-old' people (75 plus). Their book, as 'the first concerted attempt to provide a social account of language and interaction in later life', adds substantially to our understanding of old age from a linguistic perspective. It focuses on *inter-generational communication*, on the way elderly people *interact* with each other and with health/social workers, and it proposes a range of linguistic strategies to encourage interaction.

ACTIVITY 39

Write down all the words, phrases or idioms you can think of which refer to or describe old people (e.g. *wrinkly*). Divide your list into positive and negative categories, and then compare your lists with those of others in your group. Collate your findings. Is there any evidence of *ageism* and/or *stereotyping* in the group is results?

Linguistic attitudes to old age

There's a good chance that a relatively high proportion of the words in your list have *negative connotations*. Many people see the state of being elderly as *decremental* ('I'm going down hill fast!' said one old lady gloomily), as loss of hair, hearing, sight, and mental sharpness occur. This view was confirmed by Shakespeare's glum jester Jacques in *As You Like It* (Act II, Scene vii, 139). Having described the five previous 'ages' of man, he turns to the last two:

... The sixth age shifts

Into the lean and slippered pantaloon
With spectacles on nose and pouch on side,
His youthful hose well saved a world too wide
For his shrunk shank; and his big manly voice,
Turning again toward childish treble, pipes
And whistles in his sound. Last scene of all,
That ends this strange eventful history,
Is second childishness and mere oblivion,
Sans teeth, sans eyes, sans taste, sans everything.

What Coupland *et al* call the **deficit paradigm** is frequently applied to old people's *language* too. When we get older, the muscle system supporting the vocal organs does weaken, and pitch changes result (men's voices tend to rise more than women's). Nevertheless, research into older people's language skills (sentence comprehension, use of grammar, range of vocabulary etc) suggests 'only modest and qualified evidence of suppressed performance skills' (p.13). They also point out that the myth of 'old age as second childhood' (supported by public images such as road signs with stooping figures) influences public attitudes and expectations, and leads to the **ageism** we have already identified.

If people *expect* you to be in your second childhood as an elderly person, they will treat you differently from the way they would treat an adult. This shows particularly in interactional situations, and in the following examples you can see social contexts in which different attitudes on the part of the younger speaker produce different results in the old person's speech.

Extract 1

The old person (**OP**) is talking to a researcher (**K**) about a temporary home help she had difficulties with. **P** is her usual home help.

OP: ... and she told me *off* she said to me *go in* she said *sit down* I don't want you to *watch* me *washing* I said I'm not *watching* you washing I'm only having a conversation like **P** used to when she did the washing and she said *get in* then she said I don't want you watching me

K: so did she think you were angry at her and then she got angry? . . .

OP: and *all* I *wanted* was a kind of conversation as I sat down you see and yet she told me off *get in out of it* she said *get in* she said I don't want *you* watching me and of course this put my *back* up see and I come in and I sat down and I thought to myself I'll never have you again I'll rather sit on my *knees* and do the washing again . . .

Extract 2

The elderly person (**E12**) is talking to a younger person (**Y12**) about her health problems.

E12: you know yes mm (*breathes*) I think you see *when* you're getting older at this age you . . . there's a lot of things can make us a bit miserable but (*breathes*) we have a look on the bright side and

Y12: oh yes mm

E12: nobody *wants* you when you're *miserable* and *moaning* . . . thank goodness the old brain-box is still going

Extract 3

This is a conversation between two elderly people (**E9** and **E10**).

E9: (*puts on glasses*) oh that's better I don't like the light I never had anything wrong with my eyes before

E10: well well

E9: yeah till about six months ago and then it came er conjunctivitis? It's like er a lot of irritation

E10: ah ah dear god

E9: yeah never mind it'll go I expect (*laughing*) one day

E10: I get a lot of noise in my ear

E9: oh that's with our age as well . . .

What these extracts tell us is that we need to beware of accepting linguistic and ageist stereotyping of elderly people, which cannot adequately reflect the actual range of ability and skills present in this complex life stage.

ACTIVITY 40

1 Collect examples of ageist language or attitudes (look at newspapers, advertising, public information texts, and the Shakespeare extract above). Identify what aspects of age they focus on (appearance, mental capacity, physical weakness, prejudiced attitudes etc).

Write *two* short descriptive accounts of an elderly person you know well a) from an *ageist* perspective, and b) omitting any direct reference to their age.

2 Ask an older person you know ('young-old' or 'old-old') for permission to record them talking about a topic they are comfortable with (early childhood, school days, first job etc). Be prepared for them to feel shy at first, and remember that voice quality may be uneven.

Listen carefully to your recording and choose a short section (2–3 minutes) of the most 'relaxed' conversation to transcribe. Look for examples of: non-fluency features; generation-linked vocabulary; evidence of *accommodation* (ie *convergence* or *divergence*) with the other speaker.

NB This could make an interesting topic for a *language investigation*.

Gender as a sociolinguistic variable

From the moment of birth when our *biological sex* is identified, we become part of a world where **gender** matters. What we mean by 'gender' is the *role* our society expects of biologically different individuals. Although a newborn baby does not know anything more than the most basic way of communicating, he or she is beginning the journey towards spoken (and ultimately written) language as a *gendered* individual in a *gendered* world.

The effects of gender difference on language cannot be overestimated. Gender is a central, if not *the* central, aspect of the *self* and our sense of identity is closely bound up in it. Not long ago, the very idea that male and female use of language might be different, and that representations of male and female in the world might be questioned, was literally unthinkable, because it was assumed that men and women use language in the same way (regardless of their differing social experience).

In the mid-twentieth century, a hundred years or so after the first feminist conference took place in America, liberated by the contraceptive pill and by their wartime experience of independence, women began to challenge male dominance in all walks of life. More extremist feminist ideas were mocked by the predominantly male-owned press. Even so, feminist views on marriage, family life, the workplace, spread widely throughout the West and further afield, which led to important changes in public and private attitudes.

Within two decades, huge shifts had taken place not only in society, but also in the relatively new academic field of linguistics. Here a few intrepid researchers began to explore the links between *gender* and the actual *language* used by women and men in everyday situations. In the rest of this chapter and in Chapter 4 we shall be exploring *gender and language* in more detail, focusing *equally* on female and male language use.

Where shall we be looking for data? Gender issues are evident in most aspects of human communication, public or private, spoken or written, visual or aural. ***Representations of gender*** in the media (advertising, newspapers, radio and television, Internet and film) will be the first area of investigation, especially as they affect public *attitudes* to gender issues. We shall also look at **gender politics** and **linguistic theory**. Chapter 4 will continue the investigation, and will focus on *gender and spoken language*, *gender and written language*, and *gender and education*.

Representations of gender: the public domain

So how is gender represented in *public*? The first thing to be aware of is the possibility of *linguistic* and *social stereotyping* of gender, especially in the media. We shall now contrast some texts from the past with current texts representing gender.

ACTIVITY 41

1 What are the *gender stereotypes* for men and women? Brainstorm as many terms as possible which are currently (and stereotypically) associated with men and women, and write them down separately.

2 With your two lists in hand, select *two* of the following areas to investigate for *gender stereotypes*: advertising; magazines (male/female target audience); public information materials; television; the Internet; radio; children's literature; romantic fiction.

3 Look at the following texts: an extract from *The Home of Today* published in the 1930s; an advertisement from *The Todmorden and Hebden Bridge Historical Almanack* published c. 1910; and an extract from *Manners and Rules of Good Society (or Solecisms to be Avoided)* by a Member of the Aristocracy, 35th edition, 1913. How far do these texts reveal *different* gender stereotypes from the ones you have noted above?

Extract 1

From the section on *Household Management* (p.163).

Cleaning materials

This can be a fairly heavy item, especially if all or most of the laundry work is done at home. Any housewife, too, worthy of the name, is usually 'house proud', and since cleanliness is rightly rated as next to godliness, plenty of soap and 'elbow grease' must be expended to keep a house sweet and clean. It will probably be found necessary for the housewife to guard against the too lavish use of soaps, powders, polishes, etc by maids or charwomen.

Extract 2

From *The Todmorden and Hebden Bridge Historical Almanacks.*

A series of advertisements by women in business is shown on p.73.

Extract 3

From *Manners and Rules of Good Society* (by a Member of the Aristocracy, 1898, pp.107, 115, 118). There are nine previous rules.

As large dinners are ordered mainly to please the palates of men with epicurean tastes, it is not expected that ladies should eat of the most highly seasoned and richest dishes, but should rather select the plainest on the menu. Young ladies should not attempt to eat artichokes.

Ladies are not supposed to require a second glass of wine at dessert, and passing the decanters is principally for gentlemen. If a lady should require a second glass, the gentlemen seated next to her would fill her glass; she should not help herself.

AS A MATTER OF COURSE, YOUNG LADIES DO NOT EAT CHEESE AT DINNER PARTIES.

Representations of gender: the private domain

What it means for an individual to be *male* or *female* is learnt from earliest childhood as a result of observing the gender roles in the family and among friends. Learning to talk in a gendered environment, and finding out about the world (via caregivers, other adults, friends, the media) confirms these views.

Children's literature can have a significant influence on a child's perception of their gendered self: writers usually match contemporary attitudes, as we see in Enid Blyton's books, written in the 1940s and 1950s. Her 'Famous Five' (Dick, Julian, Anne, George and Timmy the dog) reveal conventional gender stereotyping; even tomboy George is represented as only *temporarily* masculine. *The Terrible Term of Tyke Tyler*, one of the best modern books for slightly older children revolves around the issue of gender identity and its representations.

A series of advertisements by women in business from *The Todmorden and Hebden Bridge Historical Almanacks* c. 1910

ACTIVITY 42

Look at a selection of children's books (your own, or at the local library) published over the last 20 to 30 years. Choose two from different periods (preferably titles you know already) and find examples in the texts of gender stereotyping. Share your findings with other people in your group.

Gender issues and children

As the child adapts to the wider world of school, gender conventions and norms of behaviour are established, and any deviation can make a child vulnerable to teasing or threatening behaviour. Researchers at Birkbeck College, University of London recently investigated gender attitudes among a group of secondary school boys aged 11 to 14 to see how they established their masculine identities. The boys' *top priority* was to define themselves in *direct opposition* to any human quality that they perceived as feminine. The result was that quieter boys, or those who had girls as friends or who showed any glimpse of 'feminine qualities', experienced homophobic name-calling (*poof, wuss, wimp, queer*). It was concluded that boys lack cultural permission to value in *themselves* the qualities of empathy and sensitivity which they *admire in girls*.

The research team felt this was an increasingly serious problem, as 'boys take umbrage at girls' burgeoning self-confidence and academic success by retreating still more deeply into machismo'. Moreover, they argued that male homophobia at school is both a cause and a consequence of boys 'lacking the full emotional repertoire [they feel is] off limits for them'.

New representations of gender

Today in the adult world of work and family, social change has produced significant changes in gender roles, leading to some gendered *role reversal*, reflected in neologisms (newly invented words) like *house husband* or *glass ceiling*. The latter term has been invented to describe the professional barrier often met by ambitious/able women. So powerful have these role reversal images become that we have *new* expectations of media representations of gender. The item below (*Guardian*, 3 April 2000) makes some interesting points:

Women are being made to look intelligent, assertive and caring in television adverts, while men often appear pathetic and silly ... [Research] showed that while women have escaped the stuffy home environment of the Oxo adverts of old, men are increasingly the butt of advertisers' jokes. In the survey of 1019 adults, 38% thought 'gullible' was the characteristic most likely to be associated with men in adverts, with only 12% thinking men came across as caring and 14% as intelligent. By contrast, more than 25% said that women had a caring, assertive or intelligent image. The image of men as beer drinking football fans and of women as clothes and make-up shopaholics was seen by 39% and 48% of viewers respectively as a frequently used but inaccurate stereotype. The group was asked about the advert for the Fiat Punto in which a man explains that the car features capacity for 94 shopping bags, 24 pockets for make-up and a girlie button for power steering. A women explains it features a navigational system, 'because if you can't find your way round a woman's body you won't be able to find your way around Birmingham'. Of those who had seen the commercial, 26% found it patronising to women and 17% patronising to men. Despite this, more than half the men and 39% of the women found it amusing.

ACTIVITY 43

1 What gender stereotypes can you find in the above article? List them. Do you find any differences between these stereotypes and the ones identified in the extracts in Activity 42?

2 List as many words you can think of to describe men and women, dividing them into *positive* and *negative* groups (e.g. *hero, princess, stud, slut*). You may find that some terms are non-gendered (*wimp, loser*). How many terms for each gender have sexual connotations? Are they negative or positive?

3 Try this gender quiz which is designed to help you to examine your own preconceptions. You are asked to decide whether the following words are more closely associated with men or women. *Jot down your impressions quickly – don't spend too long on each word!* Score 5 for 'most likely', 1 for 'least likely'.

active, adventurer, assertive, authority, beauty, chef, clerk, compromise, cook, decisive, doctor, dominant, explorer, father, hero, judge, lawyer, loud, magician, mother, musician, nurse, nurture, passive, photographer, power, private, protective, provider, public, quiet, secretary, servant, sewing, silent, soft, speaker, strength, submissive, teacher, violent, witch, writer

Social attitudes to gender

A whole range of attitudes to gender exists today, from *sexist stereotyping* (machismo male, fluffy female) to *gender role reversal* (new man, aggressive female). Extremist views have been modified, as the concept of *power-sharing* evolves. Some minor (but significant) traditions remain: *Lloyd's List*, the newspaper for the shipping trade, has decided to continue to refer to ships as 'she', by unanimous popular request; and the *Academie Francaise* has reproved the too-liberal education ministry which instructed officials to feminise job titles – apparently a constitutional crisis was threatened!

The biology of gender

What are the physical differences between male and female (apart from the obvious ones!) as they affect our use of language? The human brain remains mysterious, though we have some understanding of the functioning of the **speech centre** in the left hemisphere. Current research is investigating the role of biological difference in relation to the communications systems of the brain, but the assumption remains that the overall structure and processes of the brain are *the same* in male and female. The only obvious difference is the **vocal systems** of male and female, which differ according to age, physical structure and hormonal imput.

However, social judgements are made about the male and female voice, and as usual, *stereotypes* exist. A recently published study by the linguist Deborah Cameron (*Good to Talk*, 2000) points out that 'women's voices are judged in a different way from men's', and although her comment is specifically related to *accent* in men and women, there is evidence to suggest that similar judgements are made on *vocal quality* and *pitch*.

Because of these *social attitudes* 'women make more effort than men to change their voices; they are more driven to adapt', according to a voice-training consultant. The classic example of this is former Prime Minister Margaret Thatcher who 'went through the most rigorous training to get that deep voice'. Australian university research findings also tell us that women's speaking voices have been getting progressively lower since the 1940s, and this change is *not* biological, but about *social conditioning*. A low pitch suggests confidence and authority, probably because that's how men sound (cited in the *Guardian* 20 March 2000).

ACTIVITY 44

1 Listen to your own voice and then listen to your friends, trying to focus on the *pitch* of each voice. Make rough notes about each speaker's pitch – high, low or medium. Once you have got used to listening for pitch variation, you will be able to recognise the use of high and low pitch in voices on radio or television.

2 Listen to an episode of a soap opera or a news broadcast, and comment on the links between *pitch*, *gender* and *power* in *three* people of your choice. Present a short report on what you have discovered to your group.

3 Read the following passage carefully. Identify the male and female *vocal stereotypes* used by the author. How effective are the *metaphors* used to describe each voice?

'I don't care how many women you make love to in this room,' she lashed, scarcely recognising the high pitched voice as her own.

'Don't expect me to apologise for it.' His resonant voice had gone slightly hard.
'I hate you!' There was an unmistakeable tremor in her voice.
'Kate.' His voice was incredibly low and deep, his eyes dark and sensuous. He had never spoken her name before and the speaking of it made her aware of the deep, slightly grating timbre of his voice. It was the kind of voice suited to him, holding the gritty depths of his nature.
She gave a husky laugh.
'Love you?' he grated. 'Of course I love you.'
'What is love?' she sighed.
'Lyle,' she croaked, and was unaware that her voice came out as a wordless whisper.

He gave his gravelly laugh.

(passage cited by D. Graddol and J. Swann *Gender Voices*, 1989, Blackwell, p.12)

The politics of gender

The link between gender and politics became clearer as the 1960s turned into the 1970s and 1980s, and 'women's lib' or 'the women's movement' emerged. Betty Friedan wrote *The Feminine Mystique* (1963) and Kate Millett wrote *Sexual Politics* (1971). Feminism became linked with political activism such as the American Civil Rights, Vietnam anti-war protest movements. Concepts such as **patriarchy** (male-owned power), **consciousness raising** and **political correctness** came into the public domain. Questions were asked on both sides of the Atlantic about women's position in society, their domestic role, female education and their political, legal and economic status. These challenges (unsurprisingly) produced substantial opposition, not all of it from men.

What is important for us is the publication of two books which for the first time linked sexual politics, gender and language. These were *Language and Women's Place* (1975) by Robin Lakoff and *Man Made Language* (1980) by Dale Spender. Spender quotes the following poem by 'Astra' at the beginning of her book, and it neatly sums up her particular message.

Women's Talk

what men dub tattle gossip women's talk
is really revolutionary activity
and would be taken seriously by men
(and many women too)
if men were doing the talking ...

men denigrate our talk at their peril

but that's because they're in ignorance

of its power

our power

those previous few of us who see ourselves

as powerful

        serious

           and deadly

ACTIVITY 45

Choose any printed advertisement (which contains as much text as illustration) targeted as *either* a male *or* a female audience, and do a stylistic analysis of the way it uses gender stereotypes to persuade the audience.

Gender and linguistic theory

Following the political trend we have just noted, linguists in the early 1970s began to investigate male and female language. From then onwards, interest in the field increased rapidly, and today it is a major area of academic research. We shall look first at the development of *language and gender theory*, and then at its applications.

Development: deficit model

In *Language* (1922) the Danish linguist Otto Jespersen described *typical female language* as using **unfinished** sentences, and **avoid**ing complex syntactic structures. Robin Lakoff (1975) described *male language* as *stronger*, more *prestigious* and more *desirable*, implying that women's language **was deficient in** these features. She suggested that:

- female style is *co-operative, apologetic, subordinating*
- women use more tag questions (ie '*isn't it?*') indicating *tentativeness*
- they use more *intensifiers* ('so')
- they are more *precise* than men at describing colour.

Even Deborah Cameron (1985), arguing that women should have increased access to the language of power (male), implied that female language was ***inferior***.

Development: dominance model

The **dominance model** develops from the ***deficit model*** but places much greater emphasis on the effects of **power imbalance**. The speech of women and men *directly reflects* male dominance and female oppression, according to linguists like Shirley and Edwin Ardener (1975). They described women as a 'muted group', unable to express themselves without using male language. Dale Spender (1980) took a deterministic view and argued that men controlled meaning, so of course women could not express themselves unless they accepted 'man-made' language.

The *dominance model* theorists describe male and female speech behaviour in terms of *opposites* (competitive/co-operative, hostile/supportive, informational/emotional).

Development: difference model

The *dominance* approach had its limitations, with its insistence on seeing *all* gendered language behaviour within a power/lack of power framework. In the 1980s the **difference model** emerged as researchers investigated gendered language behaviour within the *social context* (eg the development of girls' and boys' language skills). Deborah Tannen's book on conversational miscommunication (*You Just don't Understand Me: Women and Men in Conversation*, 1992) was a runaway best-seller.

The issue of power was not forgotten, but the new argument was that women and men are *differently socialised*, so differences in their spoken language were predictable.

New approaches: the diversity model

If gender is a key aspect of human identity, male and female language use can't be studied in a rigid way. *Social context* determines language behaviour, not simply biological difference. The *dominance* and *difference models* provide useful ways of exploring human language behaviour, but the **diversity model** proposed by Byng and Bergwall (see Coates, *Language and Gender*, 1996) offers more. By avoiding *gender polarisation* and recognising individual differences, it insists on the importance of *social context* as a way of understanding gendered language behaviour.

ACTIVITY 46

Check your understanding of the theory models above by trying this exercise:

- *Deficit model* Describe any social situation in

which you have observed someone struggling to express themselves clearly (*not hearing clearly, having been asked a difficult question* etc). Try to account for their difficulty (situation, other participants, personality of speaker, emotion). Was there any question of their *language* being in any way inadequate? What might have been the reasons for this?

■ *Dominance model* Have you ever felt *powerless* or *dominated* in a conversation or exchange (with strangers, at an interview, at a party)? How would you explain this? Think about context, gender, personality, expectations.

■ *Difference model* What do *you* think are the differences between male and female spoken language? Write down two lists of characteristic features, and compare your findings with others.

■ *Diversity model* How many social situations can you think of where gender difference is *not* a significant factor? Does the speech behaviour of the individuals involved differ in any way from situations where gender *is* a significant factor? Compare your experience with other people's in the group.

Summary

In this chapter we have looked at the way language can express two important aspects of the individual self: *age* and *gender*. We have touched on theoretical and practical language issues as they relate to age, and we have explored the development of gender and language theory. In the next chapter we shall be applying these insights to 'real language'.

Further reading

Coates, Jennifer (1998) *Language and Gender: a reader* Blackwell

Coupland, N., Coupland, J. and Giles, H. (1991) *Language, Society and the Elderly* Blackwell

4 Representations of Difference: Gender

In this chapter we shall focus on three areas in relation to gender and language: *spoken language* (phonological and discourse aspects); *written language; language and education.*

Spoken language

There are two broad 'traditions' of research in this field: the *Labovian tradition* (focusing on *phonological* and *grammatical variation*); and the *feminist critique tradition* (focusing on *discourse, conversation analysis* and the *link between spoken language and cultural behaviour*).

The Labovian tradition

Labov has always seen gender as an important *sociolinguistic variable*. He explained people's pronunciation choices in terms of *overt prestige*, and identified female preference for standard forms across all social classes, as well as LMC (lower middle-class) women's tendency to *hypercorrect*. He saw this as class-based *linguistic insecurity* (but *deficit* and *dominance* theorists would see it as *gender-based*). He also recognised that mothers want to make sure that their children speak 'correctly'.

Trudgill (1972, 1983) has recognised female preference for standard usage (grammar as well as pronunciation): he also observes that WC (working-class) men prefer *vernacular* forms with *covert prestige*, thus expressing their masculinity. He noted that male and female subjects each misrepresent their own language use (women *exaggerate* their use of standard forms, and men *under report* it). We might ask whether both men and women were *conforming to perceived gender stereotypes?*

The Milroys (1981–87) identified more complex patterns of male and female usage. Women opted predictably for standard forms, men for non-standard. But whilst women had freer linguistic choice, men were under strong group pressure to use the vernacular, and especially so in economically stable communities.

ACTIVITY 47

1 Identify *either* three regional *phonological* features (e.g. omission of 'h', glottal stop etc) *or* three non-standard *grammatical* features (e.g. double negative, failure of concord – e.g. *she were* [singular subject, plural verb] etc) you hear regularly in your local area or speech community.

2 Keep a tally over a single day of the number of times you hear your chosen features used by a) *male* and b) *female* speakers. You may find it helpful to prepare a grid in advance and to work with a partner.

	Feature Nº 1	Feature Nº 2	Feature Nº 3
Male			
Female			

3 Analyse your results and discover whether there is any *difference* between male and female use of these features. Do they confirm Labov or Trudgill's findings?

The feminist tradition: discourse and conversational style

The effect of gender on **discourse structure** (ie the organisation of a continuous stretch of spoken language), **conversational style**, and how men and women choose to address each other is the concern of a whole array of linguists, coming from a wide range of theoretical positions. We shall now look at these two areas ourselves. But you should note the following 'health warnings' about research studies in the field of language and gender!

■ *Individual* research findings should *not* be generalised to apply to *all* women and men.

■ Some researchers use *sexist* methodology, where male results score quantitively higher than female.

■ Assumptions are made that male language is the *norm* (unmarked form) and female language the *deviation* (marked form).

■ Male language behaviour is often *under reported.*

■ Use of mainly *middle-class subjects* means the findings have built-in limitations.

Gender and discourse structure

Research in *discourse structure* has focused on male/female (m/f) use of **overlaps** and **interruptions**, **length of utterance** or **turn**, **topic shifts**, **tag questions**, use of **questions** and **directives**, **complex sentences** and **compound sentences**, and **incomplete utterances**.

Overlaps and interruptions

Zimmerman and West (1975) studied same-sex and m/f speech and found that in same-sex speech **overlaps** and **interruptions** were evenly balanced, but in m/f speech the balance was extremely uneven. *Interruptions* were much more frequent than *overlaps*, and much more frequently initiated by males. Total *interruptions* by men were 96%, by women 4%. Parent–child interaction shows similar patterns (86% adult, 14% child).

Zimmerman and West conclude that interruptions display *control*, are an actual *control device* and implicitly *justify* male use of control. This supports the *dominance* model.

Turn-taking

A more recent study of men's conversation (Coates in Johnson and Meinhof, *Language and Masculinity*, 1997) suggests that in same-sex conversation *men* follow the one-at-a-time *turn-taking* structure. Women in same-sex conversation adopt a collaborative, 'shared floor' structure where *overlapping* and *simultaneous speech* is *supportive* and *non-threatening*. This suggests the *diversity* model.

Topic shift

We can exert power in discourse by our use of **topic choice** and **topic shift**. If you are interrupted because someone wants to start a new topic of conversation, you may be a) annoyed because you hadn't finished, b) perfectly happy because you had finished, c) annoyed because you wanted to start a new topic yourself. 'Holding the floor' or 'keeping the topic' is a way of retaining *control* in a conversation, and evidence suggests that in mixed talk men hold the floor and *initiate topic shifts* more than women. Sometimes in domestic contexts women initiate new topics, only to be 'silenced' by no-response from their male partners!

Tag questions

Tag questions (eg 'you understand, *don't you?*') can express *linguistic insecurity*, especially if used by women. **Janet Holmes** (1995) shows that there are several *different* kinds of *tag questions*:

- questions which invite the next speaker to respond, e.g. 'Let me introduce Mary – she's an architect too, *aren't you?* These are called **facilitative tags**.
- questions which express *uncertainty* ('The train leaves at 8.30, *doesn't it?*; 'I suppose I'll have to sort out this problem, *won't I*') These are called **epistemic modal tags**.
- questions which set a challenge ('You do realise this is a punishable offence, *don't you?*'). These are called **challenging tags**.
- questions which make something more acceptable ('Never mind, you didn't mean to spill the milk, *did you?*'). These are called **softening tags**.

Holmes found that women used more *facilitative tags* and men used more *epistemic modal tags*. If men and women were acting co-operatively, both used *facilitative tags*.

ACTIVITY 48

Identify the use of *tag questions* in the following transcript. Can you invent a brief conversation between a teacher and two pupils in which *different* tag questions are used?

The following extract is from a conversation between two women – they are talking about a young neighbour who has a chronic illness.

A: there's nothing they can do

B: no she's been having treatment since she was a kid at school

A: has she really

B: yes

A: dreadful isn't it

B: it's a shame really isn't it

A: it really is

B: and she does like to do things for herself she's had several operations on various joints hips and knees – but of course there's no cure for it is there

(Source: C. Stainton *Interruptions; a marker of social distance*, 1987, OPSL (Occasional Papers in Systematic Linguistics) Vol 2)

Questions

Questions are power-related because they *require* the addressee to respond. They have many purposes (to initiate a narrative, ask for information, express emotion, maintain conversation, assume agreement) and are used often by people whose jobs gives them power (e.g. doctors, lawyers and teachers). Women use questions more than men; in same sex conversation this is a *supportive strategy*; in m/f talk women use questions to *maintain* conversation or request information.

Directives (commands)

These are speech acts associated with *power* which try to get people to do something. **West** (1990) compared the use of directives by male and female doctors. Both used them, but men used *aggravated directives* ('lie down', get undressed', 'take off your shoes and socks'), whereas female doctors used gentler *mitigated directives* ('let's see what the problem is', 'maybe we should try you on a different medication') which minimised the power imbalance.

Patients were more inclined to comply with the female doctors' directives!

Conversation structures

The **structure** of m/f conversation can vary from:

- short simple utterances with a single finite verb, often incomplete ('Did you get some milk?', 'I thought I'd – no sorry …')
- linked clauses or *parataxis* ('I forgot *but* I'll pick some up later *and* I promise not to forget again.')
- embedded clauses or *hypotaxis* ('The milk I *really want* is the green top – semi-skimmed.' 'The last time *we saw that film* you were only six.').

Jesperson (1922) suggested that men use hypotaxis (assumed to be superior), women parataxis (assumed to be inferior). Here we see the *deficit model* in full swing!

ACTIVITY 49

Can you identify the *gender* of the speakers in the extract below on the basis of their language (use of *discourse structures*)? Use the evidence above to help you.

The following exchange takes place between a commuter (**C**) and a public transport employee (**E**).

C: do you know where I can get change for $20?

E: you'll have to go into a store or something there are plenty outside of the station

C: well there's really nothing nearby what should I do?

E: what you should do is check your money before you leave home and make sure you have the right change

C: well I was really in a hurry and just didn't have a chance anyway I thought I had it couldn't you just give me change if you have it?

E: why don't you rely upon the goodwill of your fellow riders?

(Source: D. Schiffrin *Approaches to Discourse*, 1994, Blackwell, p.92)

Gender and conversational style

Research on conversational style has focused on the following areas: **grammar**; **lexical choice** and **politeness markers**.

Grammar: intensifiers and boosters

Women are thought to use more extreme **intensifiers** and **boosters** in conversation (*terribly, awfully, disgustingly, amazingly* etc). Fictional representations of women suggest this. You need to listen to people and check this out for yourself!

Grammar: use of modality

Women apparently use **modal auxiliaries** in: *directives* ('*Would you answer the door?*'); *declaratives* ('*I'd just like to say . . .*'); *compound requests* ('*When you've finished those case-notes, would you like to look at this, and then could I possibly ask you to contact his GP?*'). These might be interpreted as 'female tentativeness' (*deficit model* and *dominance model*), context-bound or as politeness strategies.

Lexical choice: evaluative lexis

Evaluative words are ones which in one way or another express an opinion. Women are thought to use more strongly positive and negative evaluative lexis ('*That's a really great outfit – you look fantastic!*' '*It's such a bad idea to go for that option*'). This usage may, however, be dependent on social context, as well as *class* and *age*.

Lexical choice: taboo language, euphemism and expletives

There are stereotypical assumptions about male and female use of this kind of lexis (men swear more than women and use more taboo language, women prefer euphemisms etc). Both Jesperson (1922) and Lakoff (1975) agree about this. Coates (1993), however, notes that their opinions were not based on evidence but on what they thought *ought to be true!* She also observes that swearing is *class* linked (MC women swear less than WC women) and that *both sexes* swear more in *same-sex* situations.

De Klerk's study, 'The Role of Expletives in the Construction of Masculinity' in *Language and Masculinity* (1997) links male expletive use with issues of masculine *identity*. She suggests that the increase of *female* swearing is challenging for men, that the gap in taboo usage between men and women is closing, and that expletive use is associated more with *power* than *gender* issues. Those who *have* power or *aspire* to have it use expletives freely (*dominance, difference* and *diversity* models).

An article on women song writers (*Guardian* 15 June 2000) comments on the way that first punk and then rock affected their work ('some of the best rock around today is by women [who] make their response to rock maleness their starting point'). Look at *two* recent lyrics (one by a male song writer, one by a female) and compare their use of taboo and expletives. Does the link between language and power, suggested above, have any relevance to your findings?

Politeness strategies: facework

Politeness is an important factor in all successful conversations. Using politeness strategies is called **facework** (ensuring that people feel supported, not threatened). To ensure people's **face needs** are met, we employ *positive strategies* ('Hi! Great to see you looking so good') as well as *negative strategies* ('Excuse me, would you mind checking your ticket – I think you may be in the wrong seat').

Are women better at *facework* than men? Holmes (1995, p.7) argues that women use more positive politeness strategies. She lists the explanations offered by linguists:

- women are concerned to involve others and make connections
- men are more detached and autonomous
- girls and boys are *differently socialised* (*difference* model)
- men and women are *differently empowered* (*dominance* model)

Politeness strategies: terms of address

Social distance determines politeness strategies like ***terms of address***. It's interesting that for most men there is little choice ('Mr' or first name), whereas for women there is broader choice ('Miss', 'Mrs', 'Ms', first name). The latter situation evolved because it was thought necessary to indicate a woman's marital status.

What determines our choice of terms of address? *Social context* seems to be the main determining factor. Using a first name can be *friendly* (ie between equals) or *face-threatening* (implying a power imbalance, where first name address is a put-down). In certain social contexts Poynton (1985) and West (1990) demonstrated that when men held the *power balance* (eg boss/employee, doctor/patient), women were addressed by their first name or by terms like 'love', 'my dear' (*dominance* model). In service encounters (eg at a petrol station) when male employees addressed women customers as 'sweetheart', 'lovey', 'dear', men customers were addressed as 'sir'!

There are variations on this usage in different parts of the world: in America, men tend to use the more neutral 'ma'am' for women they don't know, whilst in similar circumstances, women address men as 'sir'. Some terms of address are purely *male* (Australian 'mate', 'sport') and in the UK there are *neutral* regional variants (e.g. East Midlands 'duck' or 'me duck', Yorkshire 'love', Geordie 'hen' or 'hinny') addressing men and women equally.

ACTIVITY 51

Read the extract below carefully. It is taken from a *Guardian* interview by journalist Sabine Durrant (31 May 2000) with Professor Susan Greenfield, a distinguished neuroscientist and head of the Royal Institution. Durrant quotes Greenfield:

'I was in Australia recently waiting for a car to take me from one place to another and it didn't come. Eventually someone came up and said, "Oh, I've been waiting for ages, but I thought you couldn't be a professor."' She laughs, but doesn't look amused. 'Another time', she says, 'I was meeting someone in a bistro and a man said, "Oh, my dear, you look rather lost" and I said "Please don't call me my dear." It's subtle things like that. I've noticed sometimes on radio interviews if someone wishes to make a woman look small, they repeat her Christian name a lot, making her sound like a little girl.'

Use the following questionnaire to find out whether the linguistic experience described

above is unique to the interviewee. Don't forget to note the *age groups* of *your* female subjects (possible groupings: 15–25; 26–40; 41–55; 56–70).

- Have you ever been addressed as *my dear* by a male speaker in a position of power? (never, occasionally, frequently, all the time) Could you give examples of *situations* in which this occurred?
- Have you ever been addressed by a male speaker who used your *first name* repeatedly? (never, occasionally, frequently, all the time) Would you say that this made you feel small/childish/disempowered or did it not affect you? Give examples of situations where this happened.

Report your findings to the group, making sure that you correlate *age group* and *frequency* of reported usage.

Politeness strategies: compliments

Both **compliments** and **apologies** have been studied extensively in the context of gender and language. Compliments are *positive politeness strategies* which refer (directly or indirectly) to some *good* quality of the person addressed (appearance, ability or skill, possession, personality). They can be *direct* or *indirect*. For example a *direct* compliment might be paid to someone about their skill ('You're so good at tennis') or it might be an *indirect* compliment (e.g. 'The acting was superb' addressed not to the actor, but to the director).

Holmes (ed. Coates, 1997) presents a graph (p.105) of m/f compliments in her New Zealand study (confirmed by other research evidence). Women tend to perceive and use compliments 'to establish, maintain and strengthen relationships', whereas men are less comfortable about them, particularly if complimented by women of lower status. Compliments like these *face-threaten* men, in just the same way that 'stranger compliments' (eg remarks and wolf-whistles from building site workers) *face-threaten* women.

Politeness strategies: apologies

Apologies are negative politeness strategies which address the *face needs* of the person who has in some way been injured. Holmes has identified six categories of 'offence':

- *space offence* (bumping into someone) 'Sorry, I didn't see you!'
- *talk offence* (interrupting, talking too much)
- *time offence* (keeping people waiting, taking too long)
- *possession offence* (damaging or losing someone's property)

- *social gaffes* (burping, coughing, laughing inappropriately)
- *inconvenience* (inadequate service, giving wrong item).

Holmes represents the gender/apology relationship in the graph below:

She concludes that women and men seem to regard apologies differently. Women see them as *positive politeness strategies* supporting *face needs* (especially of female friends); men see them as *face saving* (to be used only when not apologising would cause more offence).

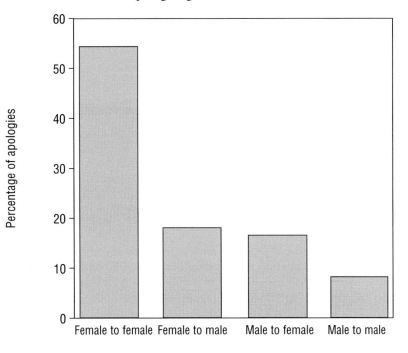

Apologies and gender of participants

Politeness strategies: back channel behaviour

Research has shown that in mixed talk situations, women use more **back-channel behaviour** or **minimal responses** (*mmm, mhm, yeah*) than men. The function of *minimal responses* is to encourage a speaker to continue by indicating interest and attention (thus fulfilling *face needs*). *Delayed minimal response* shows that the listener's attention is receding and that he or she wants to speak!

Politeness strategies: hedges

Hedges are linguistic devices which enable speakers to avoid being definite (eg *I mean, sort of, kind of, maybe, perhaps, probably, you know, kind of thing, and stuff*). Other hedging strategies include modal verbs (*could, should, might*) and verbs of state (*seem, become*). The effect of *hedges* is to weaken or reduce the force of an utterance. Lakoff (*deficit model*) described *hedges* as expressions of weakness and tentativeness in women's speech.

Holmes (1995) and Coates (1997) see *hedges* rather differently: Holmes regards women's use of *hedges* as part of their *positive politeness strategies*; Coates sees them as expressing a speaker's level of confidence in the truth of what they're saying. If women are *confident* in mixed talk they use *you know* more frequently than men; if *not confident*, they use it less. In same-sex interaction *hedges* are associated with mutual support and encouragement rather than with individual levels of confidence.

ACTIVITY 52

Record two casual conversations, one mixed sex, the other same sex. Listen carefully to the recordings, and note the use of *politeness strategies* in each. You should get enough data if you select 10 minutes from each recording.

(**NB** This would provide interesting data for an investigation.)

Gender and 'miscommunication'

In 1982 **D. Maltz and R. Borker** published a major article in which they argued that girls and boys are socialised mainly in *same-sex peer groups* between 5 and 15, that they are socialised very differently, and that these 'cultural differences' persisting into adulthood explained difficulties in m/f interaction – 'miscommunication' (*difference model*).

The linguist **Deborah Tannen** produced three 'popular' books taking the same explanation even further between 1986 and 1994. She argued that women and men belong to *different sub-cultures* and that failures in communication were *cross-cultural*. To overcome the problems, each *sub-culture* needed to understand the other's experience of being socialised (*difference model*).

Cameron (1992) and **Troemel-Ploetz** (1992), enraged by a theory which ignored research findings on women's *linguistic disempowerment*, argued that *dominance* and *power* were being ignored. Women's talk was not 'different-but-equal'; rather it was unequal and unvalued in comparison with men's high-status talk.

Today **Coates** (1998, p.415), whilst recognising that the *difference* approach is controversial, notes that current research into *same-sex* language uses a *difference* approach to m/f sub-cultures. It's even been suggested that gendered language is not biological or cultural in its origins, but evolves according to the 'talking context'. This is actually confirmed by earlier research into courtroom language, which showed that male defendants in court used many features of *'women's language'*. In other words, their *lack of power* led them to use what *was* regarded as female language, but is actually the language of *people who have no power*!

ACTIVITY 53

This extract is taken from courtroom exchanges beween the magistrate (**M**) and the defendant (**RB**) who has defaulted on his regular payments. Your task is to identify any linguistic features in **RB**'s language which are characteristically female (ie reflecting lack of power).

M: even if you can't manage – obviously you can't manage the fifteen pounds while you're out of work but you can manage something

RB: yes

M: but you've shown no good will about that have you

RB: I must admit not thinking I was expected you

know to pay any off this amount sir – I've had a job to manage anyway – and for five weeks during the summer I had sort of ten pounds a week and at last I had me fourteen pounds

(Source: Harris, in *Working with Language*, by Hywel Coleman, 1989, Monton de Gruyter, Berlin, New York)

Gender and written language

Do you write differently if you are female or male? In many places in the world, the more important question is – *can you read and write?* Literacy among women in many developing countries still falls very far short of the literacy enjoyed by men. In such countries educational opportunity is more usual for young men, and less usual (positively avoided, sometimes) for young women.

If you are lucky enough to be able to read and write, does your gender make a difference to the way you use written language? Our focus here is less on *what* you write or how *well* you write but on *how* you write. In other words, does gender affect *lexical choice* or *sentence structure*?

The writer Virginia Woolf (1925) said that:

'before a woman can write exactly as she wishes to write, she has many difficulties to face … the very form of the sentence does not fit her. It is a sentence made by men; it is too loose, too heavy, too pompous for a woman's use … [she must alter and adapt] the current sentence until she writes one that takes the natural shape of her thought without crushing or distorting it.'

So what does this boil down to in terms of grammar and vocabulary? Attempts to follow Woolf's suggestion and differentiate between the male sentence and the female sentence have had mixed success. People keep muddling *content* with *form*, deciding on one principle (men use *embedded sentences*, women use *linked sentences*), only to find in another set of texts that the reverse is true, for completely different reasons!

Ulrike Meinhof in *Language and Masculinity* (1997) tells of her own investigation of male and female writing. Male and female students and male and female academics were asked to write their responses to the request *Tell us the most important event in your life and describe it in half a page.* She hoped to free her subjects from gendered experience by focusing her question on the experience of the *non-gendered self.* Her first finding was that to the students gender made *no difference* to their writing, either in their choice of event or the way it was narrated. With the academics, gender did play a part in their narratives, but the difference was in terms of *content*, rather than in *grammar* and *syntax*. The conclusion would seem to be that gender makes virtually *no difference* to m/f use of *grammar* and *syntax* … even so, some researchers feel intuitively that there *is* a linguistic difference, but they can't quite define it!

Have a look at these two short extracts from the male and female academic texts (Johnson and Meinhof, pp.214–215) and see if *you* can identify any differences in language?

Female

I had been intensely ambivalent about the prospect of becoming a mother, indeed very inclined not to do so. I feared loss of identity and my hard-earned professional status; was dismal about the prospect of an endless round of domesticity and confinement. . . . I'd thought so hard about the disadvantages I couldn't conceive of the pleasures. . . . So when A was born I was unprepared for the joy, not of childbirth which hurt, but of her.

Male

Having children, for my wife and I, both with careers, the decision to have (or not to have) children was one of the most difficult we ever faced. In prospect one can see all the disadvantages and only a handful of benefits. In retrospect it anchors one's whole life. . . . But no words of which I am capable can express the emotions unleashed by the moment of birth, even if the male's personal physical contribution was so limited.

Gender and educational achievement

We noted in the previous section that differences in the way girls and boys *socialise together* are thought to affect their *adult language*. Both prefer same-sex friendship groups, but whereas girls play in small groups, have close friendships ('best friends'), and are skilled at managing conflict and encouraging co-operation, boys prefer hierarchies, use language to assert dominance, to attract an audience and to assert themselves as individuals. Girls and boys play different games out of the classroom, and they behave differently in the classroom.

Educational theorists are beginning to think that girls and boys learn differently, and that to ensure that all *achieve equally*, new teaching and learning strategies need to be developed. Our focus is going to be on a) the development of literacy and b) the levels of achievement by girls and boys in primary and secondary education.

Does your own experience of primary and secondary education support the research findings described above? Write a brief report, giving specific examples.

The development of literacy

Statistics suggest that by the age of six girls are reading more than boys, and that *the trend continues for life*. Despite the fact that 90% of homes have books, and that almost all parents say they read to their children, as girls mature into adults they continue to read substantially more than men.

What do girls and boys read? Boys enjoy comics and graphic novels, girls like fiction and poetry, and between 15 and 16 girls prefer magazines to books. The lowest level for reading amongst young men and women is in the 18–19 age group. Women's reading recovers from this dip, men's doesn't. Girls are three times more likely to use the public library than boys, and women between 25 and 34 read, borrow or buy *four times* more books than men. Women are sociable readers and enjoy discussion groups, something relatively rare among men.

Achievement by girls and boys

The most recent concern for educators is boys' poor performance in the literacy skills (reading, writing, speaking, listening), although the 1997 Labour government's 'literacy hour' is helping to combat this. At *primary* level in 1998 boys were much less successful than girls in the junior reading test: their performance improved by 14% in 1999, although this may have been because it seemed a more 'boy-friendly' examination, with clear cut questions and factual answers (it was about spiders!).

There were concerns about girls' *secondary* school performance in the 1970s and 1980s. In the first half of the 1980s 16-year-olds took an examination called Ordinary Level (O Level) or Certificate in Secondary Education (CSE). In the late 1980s GCSE (General Certificate in Secondary Education) replaced both.

By the mid-1970s the gap between the girls and boys gaining five good 'O' levels (A–C) or CSE (Grade 1) was less than 1%. Overall achievement in 1989 was 32%. In 1999 overall achievement at GCSE was nearly 48%, with the achievement gap now increased to 10% in favour of girls. Today, the achievement trend for both boys and girls continues upwards, but boys' achievement remains more vulnerable than girls, especially in the poorest regions where there may also be teacher shortages.

There are more concerns for educators looking beyond secondary education to m/f employment, though *Curriculum 2000* is intended to help, with its emphasis on Key Skills. Girls still have lower career aspirations, and 61% of all working women are employed in low status, low-earning jobs, following traditional gendered job stereotypes.

Achievement at school – some possible solutions

- *Solution 1* The *National Literacy Hour* scheme, started in 1998 and implemented in every primary school, is thought to be producing very promising results: as we saw, boys are now only 6% behind girls in their achievement of literacy skills.
- *Solution 2* Give books to babies! The *Bookstart* project (Birmingham, 1992) gave free books to the parents of 9-month-old babies and encouraged them to read together. Eight years later the Bookstart children are 30% ahead of their peers in English-based subjects (and 25% in maths and science-based subjects).
- *Solution 3* Make children *want* to learn. A successful Norfolk nursery

school is encouraging children to 'develop dispositions for learning': richness and flexibility in communication; curiosity; persistence; pleasure in learning and finding out about things; co-operation. Achievement so far suggests that this curriculum could develop children's learning in a way which might overcome the '*differently socialised*' experience of girls and boys.

- *Solution 4* Educate girls and boys *separately?* Statistics show that in maths and science classes boys answer 80% of the questions. Presumably in single-sex classes girls would have more to say. Other views suggest that girls' academic success *disempowers* boys. The problem is that single-sex schools can sometimes encourage *gender stereotyping* of the worst kind, so that for boys a macho climate is established with power hierarchy and potential bullying built-in. Boys may need to learn new ways of establishing masculine identity in a changing world where physical strength is not the only way to gain respect.

- *Solution 5* Adjust the curriculum to suit the needs of boys! This can range from introducing a few more adventure and non-fiction books in the library to a radical rethink – using electronic communication 'to provide disaffected boys with real contexts, purposes and audiences for writing and reading.' According to **McGuinn**, by drawing on boys' perceived enthusiasm for computers, English teachers have an opportunity to confer real mantles of expertise upon pupils whose classroom talk . . . is often undervalued' (N. McGuinn, *Electronic Communication and Under-achieving Boys: Some Issues in English in Education*, Spring 2000, Vol 34 No 1 p.54). Email communication can also be used to encourage learners (male and female) who lack confidence, and co-learning in groups in the electronic classroom can even help to improve literacy skills.

So what is to be done?

To sum up this complex situation is difficult; however, there are signs that in the field of education gender issues are taken very seriously indeed. Indeed, the various solutions described above, if implemented, could make quite a difference to gender and language issues across the board, affecting *all* the areas we have considered in the last two chapters!

ACTIVITY 56

What do you think of the 'solutions' outlined above? Is there even a problem? Note down your views on *each* of the solutions, and report back to your group.

Summary

In this chapter we have looked at three important 'real life' aspects of the gender and language issues – *spoken language, written language,* and the effect of gender on *educational achievement.* The focus of this and the previous chapter has been on how these most central and defining aspects of our self (*age* and *gender*) make a difference to the way we use language, and the way it is used to us.

Further reading

Cameron, Deborah (1985) *Feminism and Linguistic Theory* Macmillan

Cameron, Deborah (ed.) (1990) *The Feminist Critique of Language* Routledge

Coates, Jennifer (1992, second edition) *Women, Men and Language* Longman

Coates, J. and Cameron, D. (eds.) (1980) *Women in their Speech Communities* Longman

Coates, Jennifer (1996) *Women Talk: Conversation between Women Friends* Blackwell

Holmes, Janet (1995) *Women, Men and Politeness* Longman

Johnson, S. and Meinhof, U. (1997) *Language and Masculinity* Blackwell

Tannen, Deborah (1992) *You Just Don't Understand: Women and Men in Conversation* Virago

5 New Texts, New Technologies, New Uses

In this chapter and the next we are focusing on *variation* in spoken and written English in the public domain, particularly in relation to *occupation*. We shall demonstrate the remarkable flexibility and adaptability of English as a new millennium language, giving you opportunities to explore and analyse some of these variations. First we shall look at the way *new technologies* have changed spoken and written English, and then move to an examination of the *language of the media* (including fashion and sport), and the language of *business and of public information* ('government speak').

Analysing texts: a suggested model

Texts, whether *spoken* (transcribed) or *written*, have to be analysed in order to be understood fully. Whatever sort of text you are analysing (in a classroom context or an examination), remember to ask yourself these questions:

- who is the audience for this text, and what are they expecting?
- what is the purpose of this text?
- is this text like any others you know – what is its *genre*?

Answering these questions will give you a headstart, but next you must 'fill out' the bones of your analysis. Try the following questions, keeping a close eye on your previous answers [on **audience**, **purpose** and **genre**]:

- What is the text about [**content** etc]?
- What *vocabulary* and *register* are being used (*formal, informal, evaluative, technical*?)
- How is the text **structured** [*syntax, paragraphing, chronology*]?
- Is the text in first, second or third *person* (or a combination)? Why?
- How does it look [are there any important **visual** features]?
- How does it sound [is there any important **sound patterning**]?

The final question which pulls everything together is 'Does the text *succeed* in relation to audience, purpose and genre?'

Worked example

Comments in bold italic/square brackets link with model on previous page.

PRESCOTT U-TURN ON STORES CURB
FRESH CHALLENGE TO OUT-OF-TOWN PLANNING LIMITS
By Anita Howarth and Teena Lyons

The government has given backing for the first expansion of an out-of-town shopping development for almost a decade – signalling that Whitehall may be clearing the way for a spectacular U-turn over planning policies aimed at supporting city centre high streets.

The paragraph is taken from the *Mail on Sunday* (6 August 2000). It is in the financial section of the tabloid newspaper [*genre*], so the [*audience*] will be interested in business matters, and the [*purpose*] of the article is to inform and persuade. The *Mail on Sunday* often has a right-wing political agenda. The article is about [*content*] Mr Prescott's agreement to expand an out-of-town shopping development, apparently against government policy.

The extract is only the first paragraph of a much longer text, but its [*structure* and *organisation*] are typical of a tabloid newspaper. There is a major headline, a minor headline, a bye line (names of writers) and a single sentence opening paragraph. The *syntax* is complicated, however. There is a main clause (*The government has given backing . . . for almost a decade signalling . . .*), but *signalling* is a present participle with an adjectival function (post-modifying *backing*), which it also governs the noun clause object (*that Whitehall may be clearing the way . . . city centre high streets*). In other words, the structure and syntax are complex, contrary to stereotyped expectations that tabloid language is unsophisticated language.

The language is *informative* (*government, out-of town shopping development*) and *persuasive* (*U-turn, limits, given backing, curb, fresh challenge, spectacular U-turn, supporting*), matching the expectations of the *audience*. The informational language is part of the discourse of business and planning; there is no real jargon, apart from *out-of-town shopping development*. The persuasive language invites the reader to evaluate the government decision negatively, the implication being that the government is behaving shabbily.

The [*visual*] impact of the extract is characteristic of the genre – the use of bold headlines, and the positioning of 'PRESCOTT' at the beginning of the main headline equally emphasise that Mr Prescott is the focus of negative criticism. There is, however, minimal use of [*sound patterning*] (untypical of tabloids).

This is a text which broadly succeeds in fulfilling the *purposes* and *expectations* of its audience in terms of content and political bias, but which contradicts linguistic *stereotypes* about the language of tabloid newspapers [*evaluation*].

Language variation: new technologies and their applications

The 'new literacy' is more to do with *understanding visual images* than reading or writing. Children today are as comfortable with multi-modal (ie visual, verbal and aural) texts as they are with books and other paper-based communications. Most written communication in the public domain includes some visual image (logo, decorative border, illustration, diagram or photograph), and once you access electronic communication (web pages), sound is likely to be added.

The concept of *text* has changed, as we *encode* and *decode* a much wider range of communication systems today. If you look at any short text, from a bottle label to cosmetic packaging, you'll notice the mixture of *codes* (see p.3).

ACTIVITY 57

Collect up to *six* texts in the public domain, each of which includes both verbal language and visual images (eg school or college leaflet; advertising leaflet; web page; label on some kind of bottle; packaging of some cosmetic or medical item).

Look at each text with a partner and decide:

- the purpose of the text and the intended audience

- proportion of verbal language to visual image
- the kind of visual image that is being used – realistic, stylised, photograph, logo
- whether colour is being used at all, and if so, for what purpose
- how successful you think this text is in relation to its purpose and audience

What are the new technologies?

The new technologies (ICT, information and communication technologies) include anything and everything to do with computers and communication, in both numerical and verbal form. *Word-processing* was the start of the 'computer age' in the 1980s; in the 1990s computers were used worldwide, in the private as well as the public domain. The central significance of the Internet can hardly be overstated.

Other important new technologies include the *answer phone, voice mail,* the *mobile phone* and its associated developments like *text messaging, predictive texts* and *WAP (wireless application protocol)*. The development of *voice-activated technology* is producing a further communications revolution, in that people can dictate to their machines instead of writing on them; similarly voice-recognition technology permits confidential business to be conducted by telephone. There is even a voice-recognition dictionary which registers about 5000 words with 90% accuracy!

How is all this affecting the use of spoken and written English? It's worth taking a brief look at the story of the Internet first.

The history of the Internet

The Internet began in the late 1960s, supported by American government research investment, and is now the largest and most expansive system of data links in the world. It connects large and small computer-communications networks across the world, and graphically represents data abstracted from the banks of every computer in the human system. Because ordinary people can access it, it's been described as 'a co-operative enterprise with more than 300 million members'.

But is it really a *co-operative democratic organisation*? Originally a government and academic network in *public* ownership, the Internet is now dominated by the paid representatives of large corporations, and is vulnerable to exploitation. Defenders of Internet freedom argue that it must remain *mutual*, and that governments should actively promote equal access, regulate usage, and avoid restrictions on its future development.

By 2001 there will be more Internet users whose first language is *not* English, than users whose first language *is* English. Translation software is urgently needed. English is currently the language of the World Wide Web and this has powerfully influenced the globalisation of English. Machine translation (like Altavista's Babelfish version) are able to get the basic meaning across by translating words and structures according to the rules of the target language, but there can be odd results.

ACTIVITY 58

This article in the *New York Times* (20 April 2000) describes the result of machine translation. The advertising slogan for a brand of chocolate sweets is 'Melts in your mouth, not in your hands' which translates into French as 'Fontes dans votre bouche, pas dans des vos mains'. Press the *Translate* button on your computer, and this is the result – 'Pig iron and cast iron in your mouth, not in your hands'!

Choose three advertising slogans for well known products, and if you can access machine translation software, get a translation *in a language you know*. Then check the result carefully. Alternatively, try yourself to translate an advertisement slogan (French, German, Spanish) into colloquial English.

ACTIVITY 59

1 Check the meaning of any unfamiliar terms in the context of computers, and provide the full version of each acronym: some of the terms are or will already be out of date, such is the speed of new technologies!

Usenet; *bulletin board*; *protocol*; *TCP/IP*; *electronic mail*; *text message*; *ASCII*; *codes*; *ANSICS*; *hypertext*; *web page*; *HTML*; *MUD*

interaction; *intertextuality*; *IRC*; *chat room*; *cyberspace*; *cybercommunity*; *ROFL*; *BRB*; *LOL*; *IC*; *L8R*; *intranet*; *snailmail*; *cybercafe*; *Voice XML/VXML*; *Pearl*; *Java*; *http*; *WAP*

2 Write a short story or a newspaper article (300–500 words) about life in the twenty-first century, using some of the words, phrases and acronyms listed above.

What effects are the new technologies having on the English language today?

The effects are dramatic. First, a new *vocabulary* is emerging (see above). Next, *written* language (supposed to be on the decline) is reviving again – but with a difference. E-mail and text messages in particular are showing the influence of *spoken* language on *written* forms. Other technology (video-conferencing, chat rooms, voice-activated technology) extend the potential of spoken communications even further. The biggest question of all must be – is the printed book dead? Not unsurprisingly, a senior Microsoft executive is quoted as saying that 'by 2020 everything you read will be delivered in an electronic form'! Certainly full texts are downloaded from the Internet, and many libraries are going on-line (including all 15 million pages of the French National Library, translated into English by December 2000), but the printed book still seems to have its own appeal.

E-mail language

Electronic mail tends to be the preferred means of communication for those who can access it. E-mail communication differs from 'real time' Internet chatrooms, because you *wait* for a reply. Like a letter (either read on screen or printed off), it is likely to be informal in register, adopting some features of spoken language. A recent survey of 38,000 e-mails sent over a month by a cross-section of 90 volunteers, revealed that an average of 142 *messages per day* were sent by the busiest user! Of the sample (mostly aged under 40), 70% were office-based and 30% home-based: most people handled 14 messages a day. Subjects ranged from personal (around 40%) to ones concerning social arrangements (15%), work matters (9%), the technicalities of sending e-mails, using the Internet and computers (9%) and a mere 3% on topics like television, culture, politics or current affairs.

What else characterises e-mail as a new mode of communication? Apart from creating a *cybercommunity* in *cyberspace*, people say it has revived old-fashioned habits like letter-writing, encourages children to enjoy writing, and is a more gentle mode of communication than the telephone. Business people have mixed responses – too many e-mails, and the system gets clogged up, yet writing helps staff to think precisely and not to be affected by external social and personal factors. According to the recent film *You've Got Mail*, it can even be a way of conducting a romantic relationship (the 'send' message and the beep of 'message waiting' were central to the tortuous romance between Meg Ryan and Tom Hanks!). Junk e-mails (known as 'spam') can, however, be just as annoying as junk mail, even though various devices have been invented to filter out such 'block' e-mails.

Specific *linguistic characteristics* of e-mail include: informal register; uncorrected spelling and punctuation errors; use of certain well-known acronyms for phatic purposes; established conventions (*netiquette*) such as no capitals (it's like shouting), asterisks for emphasis (*like this*), and particular symbols ('emoticons') used to indicate the sender's emotional state (also used in chat room conversations and text messages).

ACTIVITY 60

1 Collect a range of different e-mails received by yourself, friends or family, on the following topics: personal relationships; making social arrangements; business or academic-related; 'block' or junk e-mails. Compare them under the following headings to see if the *topic* makes any significant difference to the *style* (language and format choices):

- vocabulary and register
- use of emotions and other genre conventions
- non-standard spelling, punctuation, grammar
- use of 'letter' style including opening and closing greetings
- use of spoken language features.

2 Write a stylistic analysis of the following e-mail, pointing out its characteristic linguistic features.

- - - - - Message - - - - -
From: Kate Jackman
Sent: 25 April 2001 11:31
To: Dave Rutledge; Jo Harrison; Kerry Hall
Subject: tonight!

Hi all!
Just thought I'd try and arrange what's happening tonight – let's get organised!! How about meeting outside the cinema at about 7? I reckon that's prob best cos the film starts at half past.
Hope that's ok with everyone. If not – give me a bell. Right, gotta go. c u all tonight,
Cheers,
Kate

Chat room language

Chat rooms are locations accessed via the Internet where people can informally exchange ideas and information, either with a group of people with similar interests, or on a one-to-one basis. They are different from *bulletin boards* (websites where people can post comments or read past contributions) and from *mailing lists* (where you have to register in order to receive e-mail contributions). Chat rooms are more social – 'you have real conversations *in real time* (our italics) with a bewildering assortment of people scattered across the planet, a few of whom give the distinct impression of having hailed from planets other than our own' (Arnold Evans, *Times Educational Supplement* 12 May 2000). Before entering a chat room you have to choose a name (or 'nick') instead of your real name (anonymity is crucial). A 'nick' should be creative, reflecting your particular interests eg 'Jazz-freak' or '*Friends*-nut'), or it could be deliberately silly or comic. As you start 'chatting' (note the *spoken language* vocabulary), you 'listen' to the conversation by watching the exchanges scroll down the screen, joining in when you feel like it by typing in your own contribution. A more formal version of chat room conversation is *video conferencing*, where the conventions are stricter, since they usually take place in a work or business context.

Answerphone language

The answerphone is more familiar than other technologies, since by the new millenium it had been in general use for a decade or so. It provides a convenient way for business or personal messages to be left when the person being telephoned is unavailable. There are two aspects to this technology – the message inviting you to leave a message, and the message left. The *invitation* can be funny, business like ('I'm sorry I can't take your call at the moment, I'm either away from my desk or on another line. But if you leave your name and number after the tone, I'll get back to you as soon as I can ...') or neutral ('This is a BT answering service ...'). Messages *left* are more varied, ranging from the personal to the formal and business like. One amusing example purported to be from the answerphone owner's fridge ('This is x's fridge speaking. Please speak slowly so I can stick the magnetic letters on my door properly').

Some people find it difficult to speak naturally when they know they are being recorded, and this can lead to non-fluency, stammering, over-formality, excessive informality etc. If the tone of the 'invitation' is friendly and encouraging, people can 'respond' almost as if the person were present, and the message left sounds like normal speech, framed by phatic features ('Hello!' 'Do ring me soon!', 'Thanks', 'Bye for now'). On other occasions the message can be close to letter mode ('Mr and Mrs Smith, this is BPS Financial Services speaking ...', complete with a signing off conclusion 'We'll be in touch shortly, then.') You can almost hear 'Yours sincerely' at the end.

ACTIVITY 61

The purpose of this task is to identify some of the characteristic features of chat room language and answerphone language. To do this you will need to download 1–2 pages from a chat room, and transcribe a series of answerphone messages (between 6–8, depending on length).

Write a stylistic analysis of both, comparing their use of spoken language features, and looking for other similarities and differences.

Text Messages

Another telephone-based technology which is increasingly popular is *text messaging*. This *written* mode of communication, limited by the number of letters available on the mobile phone face (160), is cheaper than mobile phone 'talk' charges, and offers intriguing opportunities for new ways to communicate. 'Text messaging is really different from talking ... it's a completely different thing,' says one enthusiast (quoted by Richard Benson in the *Guardian* 3 June 2000).

The formal name for text messaging is *SMS* (*Short Message Service*). Although the system was developed by EU telephone engineers in the early 1980s, it was only accepted by all the major British telephone networks in January 1999. The rise in text messages has leapt from 40 million text messages in early 1999 to 500 million in May 2000. It is hugely popular with young people in particular.

Why is text messaging so popular? It's relatively cheap; you can read it when convenient; it's discreet as no one needs to know when you're sending or receiving one, unlike using the mobile phone when you end up shouting boring and/or embarrassing details in a public place; and playing around with language can be fun (need for *abbreviation, acronyms* etc). It's even been suggested that there is a gendered effect – young men are more comfortable writing their feelings down rather than actually saying them!

Richard Benson speculates that text messaging may have a permanent influence on language ('Cd vwls dspr frm th lng'ge altgthr?'). Certainly the language conventions we've already seen in e-mails and chat room texts are essential in the confined text space available. Characteristically, tight subjectless sentences are used, and 'normal' words shortened to recognisable components. Even Shakespeare can be abbreviated ('Shll I cmpre thee 2 a smmrs day?')! Some further examples of abbreviations frequently found in text messages include: BCNU – be seeing you; NE1 – anyone; CU2N – see you tonight; JSN – just say no; THNQ – thank you; 2moro – tomorrow; PCM – please call me; I-O – yawning/tired.

ACTIVITY 62

1 Find your own examples of e-mails and text messages, and look for evidence of *written* language features (eg complete sentences). Analyse your data, using the following headings:

- SVO (Subject Verb Object) structure
- use of finite verbs
- complex noun phrases.

2 'Written English is being destroyed by the new technologies of communication.' Either *debate* this question in class, or *write* an article for a Sunday supplement, presenting the case for and against this statement.

Language variation: the language of the media

We all recognise the term *media* – but what does it actually mean? It comes from Latin and means 'the middle': so the *media* communicate in different modes *between* different groups in society. Radio, newspapers, television, the music industry, films and the advertising industry are all part of the media today, and we shall be focusing on particular language usages in each area. What is the role of the media? To *inform, persuade, argue, entertain* and *instruct* within the *public domain*. The power of the media is enormous, and increasing all the time, so we shall be exploring how language is used as a device for exercising *power*.

The media: radio

There are so many radio channels and programmes that it would be difficult to identify individual characteristics, other than the characteristic features of *spoken* language, *adjusted to match audience and programme content*. The basic functions of radio are to entertain and inform, with different networks attracting widely differing audiences, whose expectations of presenters and programmes also differ widely. The range of radio genres includes: news broadcast, phone-in, chat-show, weather forecast, documentary, soap opera, quiz, panel discussion, sports commentary, advertising slot, magazine programme – and other evolving variations of these genres.

Choose a radio genre which interests you. Listen to several different versions of your chosen genre on different channels or networks (national and/or local radio). Then select *two* contrasting examples.

How does the language choice in each match its audience? There may be some generic features in common (eg structure, content), but you should look particularly for *differences* in features like vocabulary, register, terms of address, length of items etc.

For example, the genre of early morning shows on radio includes the following; *Radio 1 Breakfast Show, Wake Up to Wogan* (Radio 2), *Morning on 3* (Radio 3), *Today* (Radio 4), *Breakfast* (Radio 5 Live), *Pete and Geoff* (Virgin Radio), *The Sports Breakfast with Alan Brazil* (Talk Sports). You could choose *two* of these to compare.

NB This kind of comparative study might be an interesting topic for an investigation.

The media: television

The language of television is as varied as in radio, although the addition of visual information can mean that less spoken language is needed, as other **semiotic** (sign) **systems** such as action, location, physical appearance, dress, vocal quality, convey meaning. Depending on the television genre (sit-com, soap, weather forecast, documentary, cartoon), the viewer *decodes* the message by a variety of means, including spoken language.

Technological development in digital, cable and satellite broadcasting has dramatically increased the number of television channels. For example, on any single day we can choose not only from BBC1, BBC2, and Channels 3, 4 and 5, but from at least 44 other channels (five channels dedicated to children, four to education, seven to 'lifestyle', six to movies, five to sport, two to news, and 13 to 'general areas of interest'). What effect does all this have on the language of television?

1 Script your own television soap! With a partner, write the final sequence (about 5 minutes) of an episode from a soap of your choice. Describe your plot and language choices to the rest of the group.
2 Write a comparative analysis of the two examples of television sports commentary below, horseracing and motor rally:

Example 1

Commentator: ... in behind them is White Emir Mungo Park hasn't picked up yet from Epsom Cyclone (.) a furlong left to go Pure Coincidence blazing the trail up the centre (.) from Sylvia Paradise then Jimmy Too Eleventh Duke is par- is going through and <u>First Mate on the far side it's First Mate now who ranges up grabs the lead over on the far side and is careering away</u> it's er First Mate who goes on to win

Example 2

Commentator 1: ... and remember when the red light comes on (.) two to four seconds (.) [race starts] and they're off holding them a little bit longer than er previously there and Richard Burns in the red car (3) now on your right hand side there he is (.) with Robert Reid

Commentator 2: come on (.) come on now Burnsie let's have it Burnsie we want I don't know he's had some small problems obviously this morning to be down in in what eighth overall but er Richard's such a nice character and beautifully round there he's kept it away from that outside edge (.) and er got the traction down

Taken from AQA English Language Advanced Paper C1, 2000

The media: newspaper writing

The world of journalism is complex and extremely powerful today; newspaper editors exert substantial influence, and myths abound about *paparazzi* and cheque-book journalists. We shall focus on three kinds of newspaper writing: *fashion journalism; sports journalism* and *political journalism*.

All newspaper writing has similar aims (*to inform, persuade, entertain*) in different proportions, depending on the format (**broadsheet** or **tabloid**) and the audience. Newspapers also have certain linguistic features in common: their space is limited and every word must count; words are frequently omitted in headlines and elsewhere; and noun phrases are often complex (*premodification*). Every story must answer five key questions (Who? What? When? Why? How?), and must lead with a *summary* of the story in the first paragraph. Any significant differences between broadsheet and tabloid tend to be in the *register* (level of formality), *vocabulary* (abstract/concrete) and *length of item*.

Fashion writing

Fashion writing can be found in a wide range of newspapers and magazines, and is intended to *inform, advise* and *entertain* readers who want to know about clothes, make-up and style in general. We all enjoy reading about designer fashion, even though it's beyond the means of the majority of readers. Below are three brief examples of different fashion writing (without the accompanying illustrations):

Example 1

Boots and bags

Here's the definitive in deluxe footwear. How about a corsage with your 6 in. spike sandals? Knee-high glitter boots? A purple velvet bag to match those silver-heeled boots? Or, best, denim lace-ups with diamante soles? No? Thought not. But at least you get the gist of the season's full-scale opulence. Remember, next time you're in a Pied a Terre, ask for rhinestones and glitter instead of sensible black leather. Glitz from the knee down, designers reckon, is the way forward – so much the better if the bag matches.

(Source: *Independent Magazine*, August 2000)

Example 2

CUT AND TASTE

Elspeth Gibson is in the vanguard of the new crop of British fashion designers. They have no time for the wacky creations of their predecessors; they just make great clothes for all sizes that are extraordinarily glamorous to boot.

[Accompanying picture]

Model approach: Elspeth Gibson (right) is something of an oddity in the fashion world. Not because her clothes are outre – far from it (main picture) – but because she insists on designing clothes for real people.

(Source: *Guardian Weekend*, 5 August 2000)

Example 3

The following extracts are taken from a *Guardian* article (16 February 2000) on fashion vocabulary and cosmetic surgery procedures:

bo-ho chic (bohemian hippie look); *radical chic* (political fashion – revolutionary T-shirts); *industrial chic* (combat trousers – functional); *capsule wardrobe* (essential clothes); *frou-frou* (rustling skirts); *fetish* (magically beautiful, *not* erotic); *candy girls* (Barbie-girl style); *equator weight* (gauzy resort clothes); *high concept* (fashion journalist lost for words!)

nose job; face-lift; chemical peel; tummy tuck; pectoral implants; liposuction stomach; eye-bag removal [prices omitted]

ACTIVITY 65

1 Analyse the fashion vocabulary in texts 1 and 2 and find examples of : foreign loan words; neologisms; slang; evaluative language; interpersonal language (imperatives, interrogatives, personal pronouns); informal register.
2 Find examples of fashion writing (for men or women) from *two* different tabloids. Analyse the vocabulary using the same headings as in Q1. Compare your findings in Q1 and Q2 in the light of their different *audiences*.
3 Write a fashion article for a broadsheet or a tabloid audience, using the vocabulary cited in text example 3 as far as possible.
4 Cosmetic surgery can be painful and unpleasant. Look at each phrase listed in text 3 and decide how the choice of vocabulary helps to make the procedure sound worthwhile.

Sports writing

All newspapers contain a substantial amount of *sports writing*, whether broadsheet or tabloid, national or local; differences in reporting style seem to be affected by audience rather than kinds of sport. Even so, football is the dominant sport, summer or winter, although rugby, golf, cricket, athletics and racing receive consistent (sometimes extensive) cover. Tennis reporting tends to be individual event-based, and swimming, table tennis, athletics and equestrian sports are similar.

Analysis of two samples of football reporting (tabloid and broadsheet)

Below are the opening paragraphs of two accounts of a 'friendly' match between Manchester United and Manchester City (from the *Independent* and the *Daily Mail* 17 August 2000).

Example 1

IRWIN INJURED AS UNITED TAKE DERBY HONOURS

After four seasons in which they have steered wildly diverging courses, Manchester's two clubs came face to face last night.

In the five years since City came to Old Trafford for a League match, which like this they lost, United have won seven major trophies, while the blue half of Manchester have won only sympathy.

United won this, too, concluding matters at the death with a crisp shot by Andy Cole who had created the opener.

This, then, was a chance for the taunts to begin in earnest, to look the enemy in the eyes and let out a little local animosity.

(Source: *Independent*)

Example 2

BECKHAM BLOWS HIS COOL AND OLD SERVANT IRWIN'S DAY TURNS SOUR

David Beckham was fortunate not to be sent off last night as he lost control in what was supposed to be a meeting of friendly neighbours.

Manchester City turned up at Old Trafford to ensure that United veteran Denis Irwin would receive at least £1 million for his testimonial match, watched by 45,158. But almost from the start Beckham displayed aggression. He over-reacted to an early challenge by City left back Danny Tiatto and should have been shown the red card in the twenty-eighth minute – sending the diminutive Australian flying with a lunging tackle.

(Source: *Daily Mail*)

Each writer starts with a different angle on the match; the *Independent* is more interested in the idea of a 'local derby' between two famous clubs, whilst the *Daily Mail* focuses on the 'human interest' angle (the behaviour of a famous player).

The language choices are interesting: both articles use **metaphor** (*steered wildly diverging courses*; *crisp shot*; *blows his cool*; *turns sour*) though the broadsheet choice may be less clichéd. Both writers use the typical war metaphor associated with competitive sport (*face to face* [implies confrontation]; *at the death*; *taunts*; *look the enemy in the eyes*; *animosity*; *lost control*; *supposed to be friendly* [implication – extremely hostile]; *aggression*; *shown the red card*). Both broadsheet and tabloid use mainly **abstract nouns** (*season*; *course*; *sympathy*; *meeting*; *match*; *aggression*), but the *Independent* uses more.

Paragraphing, **sentence length** and **structure** are interesting to compare: the *Independent* has three single-sentence paragraphs (20, 35, 21 words) and one longer one; the *Daily Mail* only one single-sentence paragraph (26 words). Conventionally tabloids are supposed to have more single-sentence paragraphs. Each sentence in the *Independent* text is complex (five subordinate clauses), and all but one (the last sentence) in the *Daily Mail* text are complex (three subordinate clauses). Conventionally broadsheets are supposed to use more subordination.

The **tone** of the *Independent* text is more humorous, and the writer uses an interesting rhetorical device (**syllepsis**) to create a lighter tone (*United have won ... trophies, while* [City] *have won only sympathy*). The verb (*won*) is repeated, its first object being concrete (*trophy*) and its second object abstract (*sympathy*). The tone of the *Daily Mail* text is more neutral, though it uses *evaluative* lexis in its comments on Beckham (*fortunate, lost control, aggression*).

It appears that both sports writers adhere in part to broadsheet and tabloid conventions, but neither seems bound by them, and style is as much determined by topic and chosen angle as by the traditional target audience for each newspaper.

ACTIVITY 66

Choose a sporting even which interests you, and select *two* newspaper reports of it (one tabloid, one broadsheet). Analyse each report (or part of it) following the example above. You may also like to compare layout, word-play (puns) and use of sound patterning (alliteration, assonance etc.).

Political journalism

Because of the political affiliations of some national newspapers (eg *Daily Telegraph* – right-wing, *Guardian* – left-wing) we tend to assume a degree of bias will always be present in news reporting. However, all newspapers have a duty to present (as far as possible) *correct information* to the public. How they achieve the balance between *accurate reporting* and *political persuasion* is interesting to explore. We shall look at the opening sentence of three newspapers on one topic, and of three others on a different topic.

Topic 1 – An administrative error affecting the pensions of widows and widowers

MPS ATTACK £13 BN BILL FOR BLUNDER ON PENSIONS

An 'appalling administrative blunder' by the Department of Social Security has left thousands of widows and widowers out of pocket and taxpayers facing a bill of up to £13 bn, MPs have found.

(Source: *Independent*, August 2000)

£13 BILLION: THE ASTONISHING COST OF SORTING OUT WHITEHALL PENSIONS MIX-UP

A massive blunder over pensions could cost the taxpayer £13 billion and trigger a flood of bogus claims, MPs warned yesterday.

(Source: *Daily Mail*, August 2000)

MPS ATTACK 'APPALLING PENSIONS BLUNDER'

An £8 billion plan to compensate people for an 'appalling administrative blunder' by the Social Security Department should be made more generous, MPs say today.

(Source: *Daily Telegraph*, August 2000)

Topic 2 – Comments on the A level results of Summer 2000

GIRLS TAKE A LEVEL LEAD FOR FIRST TIME

Girls have out-performed boys at A-level for the first time in the exam's 49-year-old history, figures published yesterday showed.

(Source: male journalist, *Daily Telegraph*, 17 August 2000)

BOYS LEFT SCRAMBLING FOR PLACES AFTER A-LEVEL SLUMP

Boys will be scrambling for the remaining places at top universities today after their performance at the top two A-level grades dipped for the first time in two decades.

(Source: male journalist, *Times*, 17 August 2000)

BOYS IN CRISIS: CALLS FOR SINGLE-SEX CLASSES AFTER A-LEVEL SHOCK

A schools expert last night called for the introduction of single-sex classes after A-level results show that girls are forging ahead of boys.

(Source: male journalist, *Mirror*, 17 August 2000)

RECORD A-LEVEL PASS RATE AS TOP-GRADE GIRLS FINALLY OVERTAKE BOYS

A-level results, which are published for 250,000 candidates today, show a record pass rate for the eighteenth year running, but boys have failed to win the lion's share of A grades for the first time.

(Source: female journalist, *Independent*, 17 August 2000)

ACTIVITY 67

In all texts, there are differences in factual information and in the use of evaluative (biased) lexis.

1 Check the facts in each text and compare them.

2 Write down all the evaluative words in each text, and identify any bias.

The media: advertising

The language of advertising is familiar to us all – we see and hear it everywhere, from billboards, television, shopping bags, and T-shirt logos, to trainers, magazines and the Internet. The prime function of advertising language is, of course, to persuade us to purchase the product. In the process of being persuaded, we may also be entertained, informed and instructed (eg advertising which includes 'scientific evidence' about a product's benefits). The range of products and services available to buy in consumer-oriented societies like the USA or the UK is mind-blowing. To understand the language of advertising it is essential to identify the *target audience*, and then to match product and language choices to that audience. Because vast sums of money are involved, the seemingly simple advertisements represent complex theorising, market research and statistical analysis. One critic suggests that today we all *live* the *advertised life*, as 'consumers living inside a perpetual marketing event', our consumption of goods linked to our sense of identity. Even our dissent is commodified!

Characteristic features of advertising language include:

- frequent use of *metaphor, simile, personification*
- rhetorical devices like **hyperbole** (exaggeration), **litotes** (understatement), **antithesis** (contrasting positions), **synecdoche/metonymy** (using a part to represent the whole), **listing**, **repetition** (including **syntactic parallelism**)
- *sound patterning* (rhyme, alliteration, assonance, puns/play on words)
- *deviant spelling*
- *evaluative language* (usually positive!)
- vague *grammatical constructions* (X makes your teeth *cleaner* and *fresher* [than what?])
- special compounds (*crunchy-fresh, yours-for-a-lifetime*)
- slogans (*make mine . . .*)
- frequently used *adjectives* and *verbs* (listed in order of popularity): adjectives (*new, good, better, best, free, fresh, delicious, full*); verbs (*make, get, give, have, see, buy*)
- *restricted vocabulary* (eg estate agents' language).

ACTIVITY 68

1 You are an advertising executive. You have been asked to choose three currently successful advertising campaigns, and to produce a short report (oral or on paper) identifying some of the *language choices* in *each* campaign which you think have contributed to their success.

2 Your next task is to produce your own campaign, using the information you have reported on in Q1, for a product to be launched on the market shortly. (Your chosen product should be as original as possible without being too way out – it should be genuinely marketable).

The language of business and of public information ('government speak')

Although there are differences between the language of business and the language of public information, there are also similarities. Business (which includes everything from billion dollar multinational companies to small corner shops) has become a management model for other public institutions, ranging from education and health to public policy and government. The jargon of business today is used not only by investment managers, bankers, insurers, computer experts and statisticians, but also by teachers, doctors, hospital managers, social workers and the armed services.

There is a built-in *tension* in business language between formality and informality. Money is serious and requires a *formal register* – the more money, the more serious. Specialised lexis, terms of address and business conventions appear in both written and spoken forms (annual reports, letters, information leaflets, strategy documents and presentations, meetings, conferences, telephone sales). Contrasting with this *formal register* is the *informalisation* of language resulting from the introduction of the new technologies. This informalisation of business language is paralleled by what has been described as the **marketisation** of language. This process crosses the boundaries between the world of advertising and the worlds of business and public information, and uses *persuasive* strategies in a non-commercial context.

The language of business also seems to have an extraordinary capacity to generate new vocabulary, some of it entirely serious, some ironic, and some genuinely useful. Well known examples include *mission statement, enterprise culture, middle management, downsizing, human resources* (personnel), *SWOT analysis* (strengths, weaknesses, opportunities, threats), *aims and objectives, quality issues* etc. More examples can be found in the financial sections of any newspaper (especially the *Financial Times*!).

Countering this propensity to produce more and more words is the **Plain English Campaign**, launched in 1979 as 'an independent organisation which fights to stamp out all forms of gobbledygook – legalese, small print and bureaucratic language'. The worst offender each year is awarded a Golden Bull by the Campaign. Encouragingly, many 'blue chip' companies and government departments have now been awarded the *Crystal Mark,* the 'symbol of clarity' for language in the public domain.

Deputy Prime Minister John Prescott (or his government department) received a Golden Bull award for the following extract from a consultation paper on the implementation of a particular policy:

... In the application by virtue of this paragraph of sub-paragraphs (4) and (6) to (10) of paragraph 3 to an application or proposed variation.

Glenn Hoddle received a Foot in the Mouth award for the following 'baffling statement' in a controversial television interview about the disabled:

'I do not believe that. At this moment in time, if that changes in years to come I don't know, but what happens here today and changes as we go along that is part of life's learning and part of your inner beliefs.'

Taken from *The Guardian*, Spring 2000

ACTIVITY 69

1 Compare the texts below (taken from business and public information documents) under the following headings: function(s) of text, use of business jargon, use of interpersonal language, use of evaluative lexis, use of abstract lexis, sentence length and complexity. Comment on the appropriateness of the language choice for each audience.

Extract 1 CHAIRMAN'S STATEMENT

The Friends Provident Group has entered the new millennium in fine shape after a strong operating performance in 1999 – one of the most successful years in our history – in which total new business increased by 79% to some £2,740 million ... the Group is financially strong, has a disciplined framework of corporate governance and internal controls, and plays an increasing role in the local and national communities in which we operate.

[Seven sections omitted]

Industry standards During the year the Association of British Insurers (ABI) announced the establishment of an independent accreditation body which will underpin the industry's commitment to give its customer a fair deal through value for money products and transparent disclosure.

(Source: *Friends Provident Group*, Summer 2000)

Extract 2 UK INDUSTRY FORCED TO PAY 50% MORE FOR GAS

British industry is being forced to pay up to 50 per cent more for gas because of booming demand for UK gas on the Continent.

Wholesale gas prices, which are paid by companies in sectors such as steel and chemicals, have almost doubled since the start of the year, causing outrage among industrial users already hit by the Government's Climate Change Levy.

(Source: *Times*, 1 August 2000)

Extract 3 HOW TO FILL IN YOUR TAX RETURN

What you have received Your Tax Return asks for details of your income and capital gains. With it I have sent two guides; this one to help you fill in your Tax Return, and another to help you calculate your tax bill (if you want to) ... *What you should do first* First, fill in page 2 of your Tax Return ... *What next* Gather together information about your financial circumstances for 1999–2000. For example, if you are an employee you will need your P60 or payslips and information provided by your employer if you have any benefits.

(Source: Tax Return Guide for the Year Ending April 2000)

2 Investigate any public institution you have access to (school, college, local authority, library, social security office, religious organisation) and ask to see their mission statement (or equivalent). Do your findings confirm that business language has become the language of public institutions?

3 Listed below are some examples of business jargon, many of which reflect the effects of *informalisation* and *marketisation*.

- *helicopter view* (summary, overview)
- *low-hanging fruit* (easy targets)
- *strategic fit* (perfect match *or* hand-in-glove with)
- *get into bed with* (be more familiar on a professional level)
- *talk offline* (discuss it after the meeting)
- *blue-sky ideas* (wild or ambitious proposals)

- *face-time* (non-electronic discussion)
- *bleeding edge* (beyond the cutting edge)
- *greenwash* (environmentally responsible company propaganda)
- *herding cats* (management jargon – something difficult or impossible to achieve)
- *infoholic* (person addicted to acquiring information)
- *multi-tasking* (achieving a number of tasks or initiatives)
- *flexecutive* (a multi-tasker)
- *presenteeism* (reporting for work even when sick for fear of losing one's job)
- *downshifting, downsizing* (sacking people)
- *thinking outside the box* (forgetting what you know)

Your task is to invent a business scenario, and to script a dialogue, using as many expressions from the list above as possible.

4 Translate the following text into accessible English, and then comment on lexical choice and use of layout.

Marketspeak Lament

The solution is

e-commerce enabled

scalable

represents a paradigm shift

is well positioned to

dominate it's [*sic*] market

Phrases emanate from my

aching brain

the pressure to accessorize

my prose always present

Without buzzwords, surely the

product

company

    service

     initiative

partnership etc

is meaningless ...

(Source: *Guardian*, 3 April 2000)

Summary

In this chapter we have examined the impact of the new technologies on English today in the world of work, and have focused on two areas for particular attention, the language of the media, and the language of business. In the final chapter we shall be exploring some of the more traditional occupations and looking at their current language use, expecting to find that the new technologies will also have had an impact here.

Further reading

Beard, Adrian (1999) *The Language of Sport* Routledge

Carter, Ronald and McCarthy, Michael (1997) *Exploring Spoken English* Cambridge University Press

Cockcroft, Susan (1999) *Investigating Talk* Hodder and Stoughton

Goodman, Sharon and Graddol, David (1996) *Redesigning English: new texts, new identities* Routledge

Maybin, Janet and Mercer, Neil (1996) *Using English: from conversation to canon* Routledge

6 Language and Occupation

In this final chapter we shall be looking at a wide range of occupations and their **discourses** (specialised language use). We have already explored the *discourses* of the new technologies, of the different media, and the world of business and public information.

The range of differing *discourses* in the world of work is enormous: in the public sector it includes the post office, local government, public transport (including *seaspeak* and *airspeak*), the Army, Navy, Air Force, law, medicine and education; the private sector includes everything from retail, hairdressing, leisure activities, to property sales and tourism. We shall focus on law, medicine and education because almost everyone has direct experience of them, and because their *discourses* include both written and spoken language. Although *service encounters* are equally familiar (going to the post office, buying tickets, making enquiries, buying clothes), these are *spoken exchanges* with many more similarities than differences (see Cockcroft, 1999, *Investigating Talk* and Carter and McCarthy, 1997, *Exploring Spoken English* for further detail).

Using **jargon** is useful to the specialist, but tends to exclude the lay person, and different occupations handle this particular problem in different ways. We shall now investigate the language of science and medicine, where the problems of specialised lexis are particularly obvious.

The language of science and medicine

There are many occupations within this area, so we should expect some varied *discourses*. The medical profession includes nurses and doctors, medical students, ambulance teams, pharmacists, physiotherapists, dietitians, speech therapists, occupational therapists, technicians and researchers, chiropodists, chiropractors, osteopaths . . . the list is nearly endless. Then there are the support staff ranging from medical secretaries to practice managers, receptionists, hospital porters and domestic staff. Dentistry and veterinary medicine are similarly complex fields in terms of occupational variation. Yet all these people have a common aim – *to communicate effectively with 'the patient'*, enabling a health problem to be resolved. Although not everyone has direct contact with patients, the aim remains the same. Hence *successful communication* lies at the heart of medical practices.

There can be huge problems in communication in this area. One of the big difficulties lies in the fact that there is usually a substantial *difference in knowledge* between the patient and the doctor or nurse, which often leads to an imbalance of *power* in a consultation. The patient feels *disempowered* by lack of knowledge. Times are changing, though, and medical education today places great emphasis on communication skills as part of clinical training. Doctors still need to use precise (and complex) terminology, but they explain more, and are less likely to attempt to exert power by 'blinding with science'. Interactive opportunities for patients like the Internet and NHS Direct also mean that patients can become better informed, and therefore, empowered.

It's interesting that fictional representations of the world of medicine are so popular (*Dr Finlay's Casebook, ER, Casualty, Shortland Street, Chicago Hope,* documentaries and hospital romance). The explanation may be two-fold: we feel *empowered* by having an 'insider's' view, and we enjoy the *rose-tinted* view of medical problems they present (all can be resolved by the skills of the white-coated or green-overalled team!). The downside of this is our often unrealistic expectations of medicine today. Nevertheless many lay people are reasonably familiar with the technical jargon of emergency medicine, which may still be alarming rather than reassuring if we hear it as a hospital patient in 'real' life!

A large gap still exists between scientific and medical lexis and ordinary people, which goes back centuries to the time when Latin and Greek were the languages of learning. Indeed, it was a fourth century Greek physician, Hippocrates, who produced the code of medical ethics which still binds doctors today. As a result, Latin and Greek still influence medical vocabulary as it continues to expand to match new discoveries. For example, DNA, the double helix code for all living matter, stands for *deoxyribonucleic acid.* The compound noun was produced in this way:

- *de-* (Latin 'taken away')
- *-oxy-* (Greek, French 'oxygen')
- *-ribo-* (Arabic 'chemical in living cells')
- *-nucleic* (Latin *nux* 'from a nut')
- *acid* (Latin *acidus* 'sour').

ACTIVITY 70

1 In a good dictionary (*Chambers Dictionary* or the *OED*) look up the *etymology* (word history) of the following medical and scientific terms. How many have Greek or Latin origins?

science; pathologist; medicine; asthma; geriatrics; paralysis; doctor; psychosis; anaesthesia; dentist; physician; cryogenics; cytopathology; cranium; chromosome; synthesis; influenza; immunology; measles; digestion; skeleton; kidney

2 Nurses and doctors – and patients – sometimes use non-medical language to discuss potentially embarrassing complaints. For example, 'problems with your waterworks' might be used to refer to a urinary disorder. Collect examples of other medical euphemisms from family and friends.

The language of science and medicine: spoken

Consultations take place face to face; treatment is given face to face; colleagues discuss cases face to face. Although so much medical and scientific information is held in *written* form, most diagnosis is the result of *spoken* consultation. What are the characteristic features of this key doctor–patient exchange? First, there is a *power imbalance* between the medical expert and the patient. This was more of a problem in the past, when doctors assumed a god-like status and patients were afraid to ask any questions, although there are still associated issues today; for example patients are less likely to follow instructions about medication if 'silenced' by the doctor's authority.

One model of the diagnostic interview has four stages (all doctor-centred): history taking; physical examination, diagnosis; management. Each stage has its sub-routines, and doctors are trained to look for *non-verbal indications* of physical illness or anxiety. Nevertheless, failures of communication can easily happen: patients are confused and vague, unable to explain themselves properly. Others mention the symptom they're really worried about on the way out, are hostile, bully the doctor (especially if she's female), misunderstand or even stop listening. On the other side of the desk, doctors can be unsympathetic, rushed, too ready to diagnose, authoritative, patronising, unforthcoming, talkative, overly technical. Today doctors are trained not only to recognise non-verbal and physical cues, but also *linguistic cues*, making successful communication more likely, with *both* participants satisfied by the outcome.

This more enabling approach to doctor–patient exchanges has been influenced by linguistic analysis of video- and tape-recorded consultations. An American linguist, Candace West investigated the way male and female doctors issued *directives* to their patients (ie a speech act that tries to get another person to do something).

She found that male doctors tended to use **aggressive directives** like imperatives ('*Lie down*', '*Just take one of these four times a day*', '*Pull off your shirt for me*'). They used **need statements** ('*I think you need to try to get out*', '*You gotta be real careful now*'); **want statements** ('*What I want you to do for me is:*', '*I want you to keep a good record of when you have that pain*'); *directive by example* ('*I would do that*', '*I'd drink plenty of fluids*', '*I'd take that aspirin religiously*'). These *aggravated directives* are based on *power asymmetry*.

Women doctors made little use of them, but preferred **mitigated directives** which were *collaborative*, giving responsibility to the patient ('*and then maybe you can stay away from the desserts and stay away from the food in between meals*'). Women doctors emphasised the idea of doctor and patient as co-partners ('*Let's make that our plan*') and did not stress difference in status, by using *modal verbs expressing possibility* (*can, could, might*). They even used *inverse imperatives* ('*You tell me if I got this*').

Significantly, West found that 67% of the women doctors' patients followed their advice; only 50% of the male doctors' patients did so, suggesting that a more egalitarian approach worked better. In another study, she found that male patients interrupted women physicians more than men, suggesting that for some patients, male gender has more clinical authority than medical expertise!

ACTIVITY 71

1 You need two participants and an observer for this role-play activity.

Using the material in the previous section to guide you, improvise three doctor–patient consultations, one *successful*, one *partially successful* and one *unsuccessful*. In each role-play the observer should note a) *power relations* b) use of *specialist and non-specialist lexis* c) use of *aggravated and mitigated directives*.

2 Identify the shifts in *register* in the exchange below, as the female doctor addresses the child patient, her mother and the video-camera filing the consultation for medical students to watch later. The child has cerebral palsy, and the mother is worried about her daughter's breathing problems at night.

Doctor: Let's see. Can you open up like this, Jody. Look. [Doctor opens her own mouth]

Child: Aaaaaaaaaah.

Doctor: Good. That's good.

Child: Aaaaaaaaaah.

Doctor: 'Seeing' for the palate, she has a high arched palate

Child: Aaaaaaaaaaaaaaaaaaaaaaah.

Doctor: but there's no cleft [manouevres to grasp child's jaw] ... what we'd want to look for is to see how she ... moves her palate ... Which may be some of the difficulty with breathing that we're talking about ...

Doctor: That's my light

Child: This goes up there.

Doctor: It goes up there. That's right ... Now while we're examining her head we're feeling for lymph nodes in her neck ... or for any masses ... okay ... also if you palpate the midline for thyroid, for goiter ... if there's any ... Now let us look in your mouth. Okay? With my light. Can you open up real big? Oh, bigger ... Oh bigger ... Bigger.

(Source: D. Tannen (ed.) *Framing in Discourse*, 1993, OUP pp.64–5)

The language of science and medicine: written

Written language in the field of science and medicine includes research articles, prescriptions, leaflets, medication instructions, web pages, text books, scientific and medical journalism, medical dictionaries, and case notes. In many of these genres, accessibility of language is an issue for non-specialists.

Scientific writing for non-specialists

In the field of science, the 'intelligibility gap' is being bridged by distinguished scientists like Stephen Hawking (*A Brief History of Time*), Richard Dawkins (*The Selfish Gene* and *The Blind Watch-maker*) and Susan Greenfield (*The Brain*), who write fluently about astrophysics, human genetics and neurology. They have found ways of addressing the basic problem that complex ideas tend to be expressed in complex language.

The following extract is taken from Hawking's *A Brief History of Time* (1998, p.10):

It turns out to be very difficult to devise a theory to describe the universe all in one go. Instead, we break the problem up into bits and invent a number of partial theories. Each of these partial theories describes and predicts a certain limited class of observations, neglecting the effects of other quantities, or representing them by simple sets of numbers. It may be that this approach is completely wrong. If everything in the universe depends on everything else in a fundamental way, it might be impossible to get close to a full solution by investigating parts of the problem in isolation. Nevertheless it is certainly the way we have made progress in the past.

ACTIVITY 72

Analyse the text above, looking for examples of the following: shorter sentences; a balance between abstract and concrete nouns; careful cohesion (lexical cohesion and metadiscourse like *firstly, next, moreover*); avoidance of lengthy noun phrases; moderate use of passive constructions; avoidance of too many abstract nouns.

Scientific journalism

Many broadsheet newspapers regularly publish items on science and medicine which also bridge the intelligibility gap. The texts below are good examples of the genre.

ROCKET FUEL FROM THIN AIR

A flash of light on a specially prepared plastic plate can turn nitrogen from the air into solid rocket fuel, say Japanese scientists. Their discover could lead to a new process for making not just rocket fuel, but other important nitrogen compounds, such as fertilisers, pharmaceuticals and explosives.

(Source: *Guardian*, 3 August 2000)

LIFE IN THE TIME OF CHOLERA

It [the cholera bacterium] can survive peacefully in a saltwater estuary, but it can kill a human being in a day. It can live for days in water aboard a ship or a railway carriage, and it can survive for two weeks inside the warm water inside the hump of a camel. There are even humans who can carry Vibrio cholerae in their guts and suffer no symptoms. But these dangerous people – they can spread the infection without knowing it – are very few indeed.

(Source: *Guardian*, 3 August 2000)

ACTIVITY 73

Choose a scientific topic or medical issue which interests you, and write a short article (500–1000 words) for a broadsheet audience, using the accessible style you have studied above. Notice in the *Guardian* extracts above the use of rhetorical patterns like triple structures (*fertilisers, pharmaceuticals and explosives*) and antithesis (*... survive peacefully, but ... can kill*).

Medical writing to advise, inform and instruct

Most of us are familiar with healthcare leaflets available at doctors' surgeries, and in hospital waiting areas. Specific leaflets may be given to patients who have a particular medical problem, or who are to have surgery. The aim is to be clear, informative, patient-friendly and accessible – the influence of the Plain English Campaign again. The example below, taken from a Surgical Information Sheet given to patients who 'may have a form of cancer', explains the sheet's purpose:

You will probably be upset by the news and may well have forgotten much of what he [the surgeon] discussed with you. This leaflet will answer many of your questions.

Other leaflets have been similarly revised, and the user-friendly style has even percolated through to a local authority primary health care group:

WE ARE NOW PROPOSING TO BECOME AN NHS TRUST ... AND WE WELCOME YOUR VIEW
(Source: Broxtowe and Hucknall NHS Primary care group leaflet)

Dentists have followed suit. NHS dental care acceptance forms explain 'What NHS dental care means for you' under a variety of headings, including the following:

Emergency arrangements Whenever possible please contact us about emergencies during normal surgery hours. If you need to be seen the same day please get in touch as early in the day as possible. If an emergency arises out of hours, telephone the surgery for advice. If treatment is necessary, we will do our best to arrange it within 24 hours.

Information leaflets accompanying medications have also been revised by the pharmaceutical companies. Layouts are simpler, using subheadings and visual images (multi-modal texts!). The language is direct and friendly:

WHAT YOU NEED TO KNOW ABOUT YOUR INHALER

Patient Information

Please ready this carefully before you start to use your medication. If you have any questions or are not sure about anything ask your doctor or pharmacist.

How to use your Inhaler

If this is a new inhaler or you have not used the inhaler for two weeks or more, it must be tested before use by releasing four puffs into the air.

1 Remove the cover from the mouthpiece, and shake the inhaler vigorously.

2 Holding the inhaler as shown, breathe out gently (but not fully) and then immediately place the mouthpiece in your mouth and close your lips around it.

ACTIVITY 74

Analyse the ways in which the extracts above have been made user-friendly, focusing particularly on the use of interpersonal language.

The language of law

Law functions everywhere: in Parliament, at the supermarket, in the courtroom, on the M25, at the hairdresser's, at college, the estate agency and the doctor's surgery. Yet most of the time we are unaware of its existence – until we have a problem. Then the network of the legal system (police, magistrates, legal executives, solicitors, barristers, clerks of chambers) reveals itself. There are different kinds of legal language: the language of the *legislature* (*Parliamentary*); the language of the *judiciary* (who interpret and apply parliamentary law); the language of *legal documents* (property deeds, wills etc); the language of *legal reference texts*; and the language of *case law* (judges' decisions on individual cases).

The language of law and the language of everyday life are radically different. The vocabulary of *written* law (deriving from Roman and French, as well as Old English law) contains many fossilised forms, such as:

- *affadavit*; *alibi*; *jurisprudence*; *sui juris* (Latin)
- *plaintiff*; *counsel*; *tort*; *estoppel*; *fee simple* (French)
- *whereby*; *witnesseth*; *hereinto*; *thereafter*; *aforesaid*; *theretofore* (Old English).

These forms have survived because legal language needs to be *precise, coherent* and *unambiguous*, and these terms have particular and important meaning. Since the law is 'a profession of words' (Melinkoff), respect for legal tradition is important, but it also remains important that excessive wordiness, pomposity and lack of clarity should be avoided.

ACTIVITY 75

The language of law is easy to find: legal notices in newspapers; bus pass or railcard; house deeds and tenancy agreements; insurance documents, hire purchase agreements; birth, marriage or death certificates.

As a supporter of the Plain English Campaign, rewrite a legal document of your choice in *simplified* form.

Spoken legal language

Spoken legal language is the language of the courtroom with all its formal procedures and rules. David Crystal describes it as a giant narrative with beginning (*opening statements*), middle (*evidence*) and end (*closing arguments* and *verdict*). The story is told by many people – and there are always two conflicting versions (prosecution and defence).

Although there is some *ceremonial language* involved ('*Your Honour*', '*May it please the court*', '*The truth, the whole truth and nothing but the truth*') most courtroom language is the everyday language used by witnesses, lawyers, and judge to inform the jury. (Other examples of spoken language in a legal context include recorded and transcribed police interviews, and lawyers' statements to the press.) The following examples of courtroom language clearly show *non-specialised lexis*.

(**M** is the magistrate, **C** the clerk and **DH** the defendant in text 1, **RA** the defendant in text 2):

Text 1

M: why haven't you been paying more than this – what – will you give us a reason?

DH: well actually your worships like I've uh you know about a year and a half ago I fell out of – well – my wife left me like – and I've been all – you know I just started drinkin' and that like and uh – go to the pub one night and seen her and we've got back together again now so

M: but you see – you've committed this offence – and this is a *commitment – a court* commitment and – you should of – have been paying this – it's no excuse that you've just had domestic troubles and gone off drinking and things – this should have been as I understand it there's been nothing paid – in the last six months of last year – is that right Mr – [to the clerk]

Text 2

M: well if you flatly refuse to *accept* the order of the court there's only one alternative – then you'll go to prison

RA: yeh

M: is that what you're saying

RA: yes

M: will you fetch a policeman [to the usher]

RA: you can't do it now uh I'm still under psychiatric treatment

M: you can receive that in prison Mr – uh **A**

RA: oh thank you [with ironic intonation]

M: you can't tell – you can't refuse to do something and tell us what we can do at the same time you know

RA: that's the system in't it

(Source: Harris, cited in *Working with Language*, by Hyweth Coleman, 1989 Mouton de Gruyter, Berlin, New York p.80)

ACTIVITY 76

1 The extracts above represent the everyday nature of magistrate–defendant exchanges. How does the language of each reveal their attitude to the courtroom situation? (Look at lexis, spoken language features.)
2 Courtroom scenes on television or film are relatively accessible. Find an example of courtroom drama to watch, and see how far the 'effective courtroom strategies' described by Crystal are used in this fictional version.

- Is the questioning varied?
- Have the witnesses on one side been given more chance to speak at length than the others during cross-examination?
- Are the lawyers remaining poker-faced throughout?
- Is the jury interested, rather than bored?
- Is repetition being used appropriately (don't bore the jury)?
- Are witnesses speaking uninterrupted (don't seem to want to conceal facts)?
- Are objections being used sparingly?

Written legal language

Because law is based on 'words', the written word is central to every aspect of its functioning, and includes everything from case law records and signed police statements to law reports, legal journalism, written judgements, Acts and Statutes and local bye-laws. Different legal contexts require specialised lexis, but there are some recognisable characteristics.

We've already noted the archaic vocabulary, but there are other older usages, such as **repetition of meaning** (*each and every, have and hold, null and void, will and testament*) and **specialised words** (*appeal, bail, defendant, libel*). Then there are lawyers' **discussion language** (*issue, strike from the record, objection, alleged*) and deliberately **vague terms** (*adequate cause, reasonable care, undue interference, nominal sum*) contrasted with extremely **precise and unchangeable words** (*irrevocable, in perpetuity*).

From the viewpoints of layout and grammar, legal documents generally lack *punctuation*, use *modal* verbs precisely (*must* means legal **obligation**, *may* means legal **possibility**) and prefer lengthy sentences including long lists to ensure *precise* meaning is established.

However, change is underway in the language of the law, both spoken and written. In April 1999, the Lord Chancellor's Department (with the assistance of the Plain English Campaign) replaced much archaic and repetitive language with more accessible 'plain English'. The aim has been to ensure that the process of civil justice should move as *rapidly* and *transparently* as possible. For example:

- *plaintiff*   becomes *claimant*
- *writ*   becomes *claim*
- *discovery*   becomes *disclosure of evidence*
- *in camera*   becomes *private*
- *minor/infant*   becomes *child*
- *subpoena*   becomes *witness summons*
- *guardian ad litem* becomes *litigator's friend*
- *ex parte*   becomes *without notice of the hearing*
- *inter partes*   becomes *on notice of a hearing.*

According to the Director of the Open University Law Programme (*Open Eye 2000*, p.20), many lawyers were caught out by the changes, including a High Court barrister. On the morning the rules came into effect, he addressed the presiding judge and declared, 'My Lord, I appear for the plaintiff in this action.' The judge's reply was withering. 'No you don't, you appear for the claimant.'

ACTIVITY 77

Look at the following examples of legal language (a law report of a judgement, and an application for a licence). Compare the use of legal language in each text, and identify as many characteristic features as possible, using the descriptors above to help you.

Law report

Queen's Bench Division (published August 1 2000) REGINA V. GOVERNOR OF FRANKLAND PRISON, EX PARTE RUSSELL AND ANOTHER Before Mr. Justice Lightman. *Judgment July 10, 2000*

While a prison officer could properly lay down conditions regulating access to the place where food was provided, could order prisoners to comply with such conditions and could treat disobedience to such an order as a disciplinary offence, neither such conditions nor the failure of a prisoner to comply with them could excuse the governor from the obligation to provide adequate food to the prisoner.

[The prisoner had refused to wear prison clothes when confined to his cell; the governor had refused to allow him to collect food from the servery wearing only a blanket, and had sent only one meal a day to the cell. The judge ruled that the governor, whatever the breach of discipline, must provide adequate food to the prisoner.]

Legal notice

PETTY SESSIONAL DIVISION OF SOUTH WEST SURREY NOTICE OF APPLICATION PROVISIONAL JUSTICES ON-LICENCE TO WHOM IT MAY CONCERN

I, I . . . G . . . c/o . . ., High Street . . . having in the past six months carried on the trade or calling of Company Director DO HEREBY GIVE YOU NOTICE that it is my intention to apply at the transfer sessions for the petty Sessional division of South West Surrey to be held at Guildford Magistrates Court, The Court House, Mary Road, Guildford on 1 September 2000 at 10.00 am for the grant to me of a provisional licence authorising me to sell by retail intoxicating liquor of all descriptions for consumption on and off the premises about to be altered and situate at . . . and to be known by the sign of . . . which said premises are owned by . . . AND FURTHER TAKE NOTICE that this licence shall be subject to conditions deposited with the Clerk to the Licensing Justices.

Forensic linguistics

Forensic linguistics is a relatively new area of the law which links the science of linguistics with legal language (spoken or written). A classic example of this was the case of Derek Bentley, the young man who was hanged for the murder of a policeman, committed by someone else 'who was under age at the time'. The story of Bentley's hanging is told in the film *Let Him Have It*. The discourse analyst, Malcolm Coulthard, was able to show that the educationally sub-normal Bentley could not have used the lexis or the complex syntax of his alleged confession. It was partly his statement, partly the result of the interview and partly the policeman's own writing. The beginning of the confession is quoted below:

I have known Craig since I went to school. We were stopped by our parents going out together, but we still continued going out with each other – I mean we have not gone out together until tonight. I was watching television tonight (2 November 1952) and between 8 pm and 9 pm, Craig called for me. My mother answered the door and I heard her say I was out. I had been out earlier to the pictures and got home just after 7 pm. . . . When we came to the place where you found me, Chris [Craig] looked in the window. There was a little iron gate at the side. Chris then jumped over and I followed. Chris then climbed up the drainpipe to the roof and I followed . . . Then someone in the garden on the opposite side shone a torch up towards us. Chris said: 'It's a copper, hide behind here' . . . We were there waiting for about ten minutes. I did not know he was going to use the gun. A plain clothes man climbed up the drainpipe and on to the roof. The man said: 'I am a police officer – the place is surrounded.' He caught hold of me and as we walked away Chris fired.

(Source: Coulthard in *Advances in Spoken Discourse Analysis*, 1992, Routledge, p.242)

Forensic linguists are called on today to provide expert evidence about accent, dialect, language interference, voice prints, and even to analyse the language of suicide notes in relation to differing cultural expectations.

ACTIVITY 78

You may like to try your own forensic linguistic analysis of the extract from Bentley's confession (eg look at register, sentence structure, use of negatives, standard/non-standard English usage).

As a result of many years of appeals by his family and other supporters, Derek Bentley was posthumously pardoned by the Queen in July 1998.

The language of education

The world of education is very familiar to most of us today, whether as pupil, student, teacher, lecturer or parent. What makes the *language of education* different from everyday language? The differences are less obvious than in the fields of law and medicine; nevertheless the *discourses* of different educational institutions and their management can vary widely (compare managing a nursery with running a university). Similarly, *educational theory* has its own *discourse* (subject-related), as does classroom practice. Then there are the *discourses* of national education policy-makers, politicians, school governors, teacher training establishments and distance learning institutions (eg the Open University). Many universities have their own educational *discourse* in relation to their teaching and learning strategies. Examination boards, examiners and markers have their own *discourse*, and so does the Inspectorate, whose purpose is to improve quality and raise standards by encouraging good practice and discouraging poor performance. We can conclude that the language of education is astonishingly complex in its range of *discourses*.

The aim of education is to enable all learners to achieve their potential. For adults as well as children this means acquiring communicative competence in four areas:

- **grammatical competence** (learning and internalising the structures of language)
- **discourse competence** (ability to understand and create longer stretches of spoken and written language)
- **strategic competence** (ability to monitor and self-correct own language)
- **sociolinguistic competence** (ability to use language in varied social situations, adapting register etc)

The most effective way to learn is to take responsibility for your own learning, as far as possible. A teacher has to find ways of involving individuals in their own learning, acting sometimes as instructor, sometimes as coach, at all times aware of individual needs, as well as external factors affecting their learning, such as gender, ethnicity, social class, or bilingualism. Language has a hugely important part to play in all this, and we shall look at three particular areas – *classroom language, ICT and education*, and the *Literacy Hour*. We shall conclude with an appalled glance at educational jargon.

Classroom language

The language of the classroom is predominantly spoken, though written language is present in texts and in the students' and teachers' own work. The basic structure of teacher–pupil exchange is **Initiation Response Feedback (IRF)**, first described by the linguists **John Sinclair** and **Malcolm Coulthard** in 1975. An example of IRF follows:

Teacher: Who remembers what water is made of? (*Initiation*)

Pupil 1: Hydrogen and oxygen (*Response*)

Teacher: Good, well remembered (*Feedback*) Now I wonder if you can remember the proportions of oxygen and hydrogen? (*Initiation*)

Pupil 2: I think it's two parts oxygen, one part hydrogen …? (*Response*)

Teacher: Not quite right – it's the other way round – two parts hydrogen, one part oxygen (*Feedback*). Never mind – you won't forget next time.

One problem that can arise with the use of IRF exchanges is that the emphasis for pupils is on providing 'answers' all the time, which *breaks up* rather than *consolidates* their learning. Another problem is over-use of *closed questions* (the teacher knows the 'right' answer), whereas *open questions* (the teacher *wants to hear* the pupil's view) produce more coherent learning.

Collaborative learning is another classroom strategy, sometimes teacher-directed (*please discuss these questions in small groups and report back*), sometimes entirely pupil-directed (*let's discuss this question*). The latter requires the establishment of an agreed structure for talk in order to be successful – but it is one of the most effective ways of learning.

ACTIVITY 79

With permission, tape-record the whole or part of an A level lesson. Analyse the use of IRF exchange structures, and other classroom strategies. Notice the use of feedback and evaluation by teacher and fellow students. Note too the use of phatic language, terms of address and evaluative lexis.

The effects of ICT on the language of education

Although not all teachers have quite caught up with the ICT revolution, most are keen to use it to support their teaching and their students' learning. The new technology has huge potential to help learners at all levels, ranging from virtual seminars and international curriculum collaboration to national library websites and specialist software for children with learning difficulties. Learners can be taught as individuals within the inclusive and 'boundary-less classroom' which ICT offers. The real possibility of personal success can be offered to children unused to achieving. Language skills development seems a fruitful area of ICT, particularly with the use of interactive software. The use of electronic texts to develop creative writing or specialised websites supporting dyslexic students confirms the potential of ICT to enrich all aspects of the language of education.

ACTIVITY 80

How much has ICT benefited you in the course of your education? Find an example of a website relevant to your A level studies, and assess its effectiveness as a teaching and learning tool.

Write an article for your local paper about the usefulness of ICT in education, referring particularly to your own observation.

Literacy development

The introduction of the **Literacy Hour** is one of the most successful recent initiatives in primary education. Reading is taught using **phonics** (sounding each *phoneme*), which enables children to see how written language works at *word, sentence* and *text* levels. There have been nationwide improvements in children's reading skills (SAT tests); the next target is to improve children's *writing skills* (hardest of all to master).

The extract below tells us some of the skills literate primary pupils should have. They should:

- be able to read and write with confidence, fluency and understanding
- be able to orchestrate a full range of reading cues (phonic, graphic, syntactic, contextual) to monitor their reading and correct their own mistakes
- understand the sound and spelling system and use this to read and spell accurately
- have an interest in words and their meanings and a growing vocabulary
- know, understand and be able to write in a range of genres in fiction and poetry
- understand, use and be able to write a range of non-fiction texts
- plan, draft, revise and edit their own writing
- through reading and writing, develop their powers of imagination, inventiveness and critical awareness.

ACTIVITY 81

1 If possible, get permission to go into a local primary school to observe the Literacy Hour in action. Note what language point the teacher is focusing on, what strategies are used, and how the children respond. Give a brief oral report of your findings to the group.

2 It has been suggested that young writers have difficulties with the following: getting the 'feel' of a sentence and mastering punctuation; knowing when and how to add detail and description and when to use pronouns to avoid repetition; how to vary their sentence construction, especially openings; using a *variety* of connectives (*when, after, several days later*) instead of *and, then*.

Choose three examples of primary children's creative writing (your own, a brother's or sister's, or from your local school) to examine. Is there evidence to support the claims above? Choose *one* problem area, and plan a teaching strategy to help primary children to overcome this problem.

The language of education: jargon

One of the problems of new developments in any field is the inexorable growth of *jargon*. Education (like law, a profession where words really do count!) has always been jargon-ridden, but it's getting worse. The *discourse of education* may be in danger of verbal-suffocation. Look at the examples below:

- QAA, QCA, AQA, OCR, UCAS, EDEXCEL, AS, FEFC, GNVQ, DFEE
- *promote high quality teaching and learning*
- *significantly raise standards in literacy and numeracy*
- *join schools together in a dynamic partnership*
- *strategic intent*
- *raising expectations*
- *empower*
- *secure a climate of continual improvement*
- *frontiers of learning.*

Even educational experts find it hard not to use jargon: a Birmingham University professor won a Golden Bull award (Plain English Campaign) for the title of a research project: *The Measurement of Consumer Criteria for Manufacturer Parameter Values in Biscuit Texture* (actual topic – whether crunchy biscuits taste nice). Elsewhere it has been remarked 'Teaching isn't allowed any more, only facilitating learning outcomes'.

We hope this isn't true.

Summary

This chapter has focused on language and occupation in three specific fields: *science and medicine, law* and *education.* In all these areas the interaction of language and society is crucial, and has been flagged up wherever possible. We hope that reading the book has enabled you to look deeper and to understand more about the way we use spoken and written language in every aspect of our lives. Our idiolect reflects not only our individual self, but also ourselves as members of human, global society.

Further reading

Carter, Ron and McCarthy, Mike (1997) *Exploring Spoken English* Cambridge University Press

Coates, Jennifer (ed.) (1998) *Language and Gender* Blackwell

Cockcroft, Susan (1999) *Investigating Talk* Hodder and Stoughton

Coleman, Hywel (ed.) (1989) *Working with Language: a Multi-Disciplinary Consideration of Language Use in Work Contexts* Mouton de Gruyter

Coulthard, Malcolm (ed.) (1992) *Advances in Spoken Discourse Analysis* Routledge

Hawking, Stephen (1998) *A Brief History of Time* Bantam Press

Tannen, Deborah ed. (1993) *Framing in Discourse* Oxford University Press